Battles of Ancient China

Battles of
Ancient China

Chris Peers

Pen & Sword
MILITARY

First published in Great Britain in 2013 by
Pen & Sword Military
an imprint of
Pen & Sword Books Ltd
47 Church Street
Barnsley
South Yorkshire
S70 2AS

ISBN 978 1 84884 790 3

Typeset in Ehrhardt by
Mac Style, Driffield, East Yorkshire
Printed and bound in the UK by CPI Group (UK) Ltd, Croydon,
CRO 4YY

Pen & Sword Books Ltd incorporates the imprints of Pen & Sword
Archaeology, Atlas, Aviation, Battleground, Discovery, Family History,
History, Maritime, Military, Naval, Politics, Railways, Select, Social
History, Transport, True Crime, and Claymore Press, Frontline Books,
Leo Cooper, Praetorian Press, Remember When, Seaforth Publishing
and Wharncliffe.

For a complete list of Pen & Sword titles please contact
PEN & SWORD BOOKS LIMITED
47 Church Street, Barnsley, South Yorkshire, S70 2AS, England
E-mail: enquiries@pen-and-sword.co.uk
Website: www.pen-and-sword.co.uk

Contents

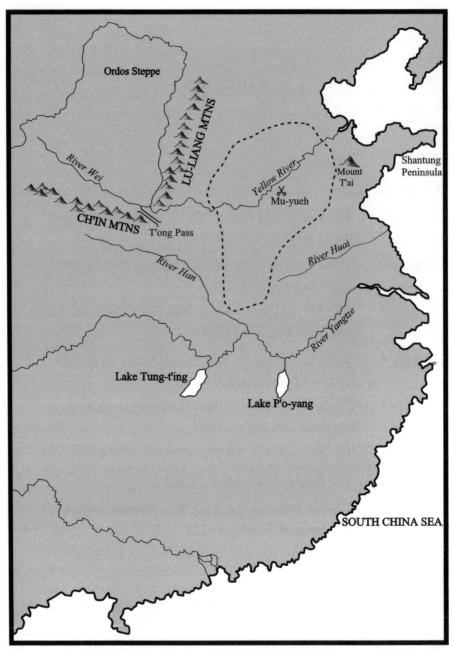

The main geographical features of ancient China. The dotted line denotes the approximate extent of the Shang kingdom before its overthrow at the hands of the Chou in the eleventh century BC.

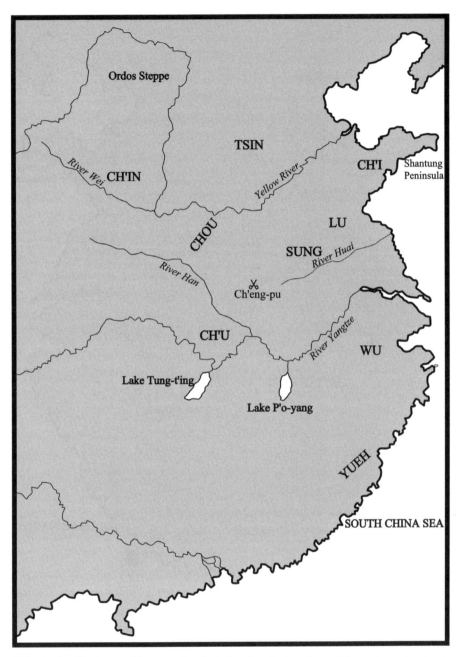

China in the 'Springs and Autumns' period, showing the locations of the main contenders in the wars of the seventh century BC.

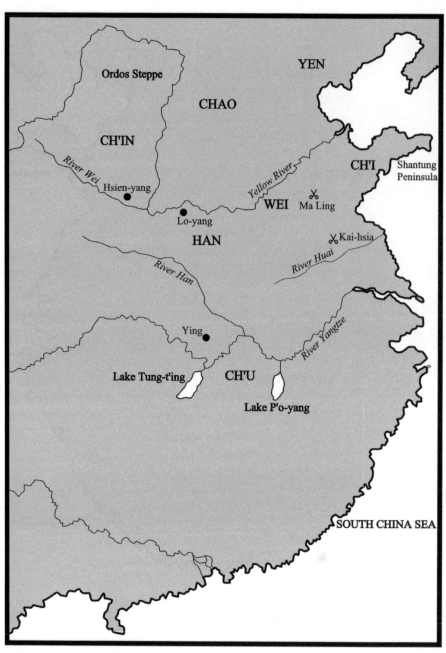

The 'Warring States', c. 300 BC.

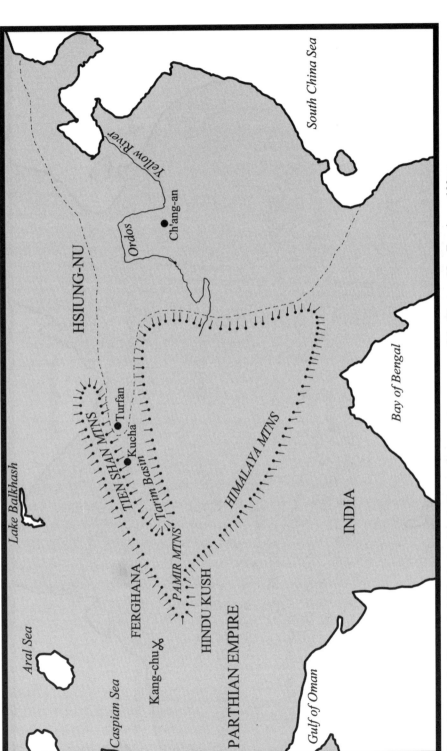

Central Asia in the Han period. The broken line indicates the approximate extent of the Western Han Empire, c. 100 BC.

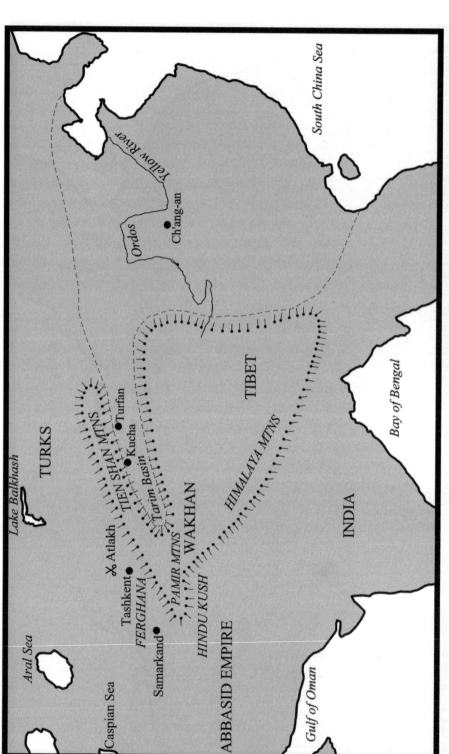

Central Asia in the T'ang period. The broken line indicates the approximate extent of the T'ang Empire, c. AD 750.

Introduction

Ancient China: History and Myth

In the following chapters I intend to illustrate the evolution of the military art in ancient and medieval China with reference to ten battles or series of battles, and the campaigns which gave rise to them. They represent only a tiny fraction of the full scope of Chinese military history, but have been selected both for their historical importance and for the light which they shed on the weapons and tactics of the time. However the choice is also constrained by the limitations of the available sources. Chinese historical writing has been strongly influenced by the anti-military tradition which we associate with the great philosopher Confucius, and in the past many scholars did not consider the minutiae of military operations worth recording. There are several notable exceptions, but their coverage of events is often patchy, with the result that we can reconstruct a number of fairly minor actions in considerable detail, while our sources remain frustratingly vague about what we would regard as the pivotal events of the wars in question. For example, the relatively minor skirmish between Han troops and Hsiung-nu 'barbarians' at Kang-chu in 36 BC is recounted at greater length than the far more extensive campaigns of Huo Ch'u-p'ing and others against the Hsiung-nu between 121 and 119 BC – not because it was necessarily of greater historical significance, but because, as Michael Loewe points out in his study of military operations under the Han dynasty, Huo's campaign went entirely according to plan, and so was subjected to less thorough analysis in official documents.

It is perhaps not surprising, in view of the linguistic and cultural barriers, that – despite its recent rise to prominence on the world stage – China remains a land of mystery to many in the west. A remarkable number of myths about Chinese history are still current. Of these, by

xii   Battles of Ancient China

far the most enduring concerns the Great Wall. In recent years several excellent studies, some of which are cited in the Bibliography, have tried to put this iconic structure into its true perspective, but it is still not uncommon to find popular works treating the Wall as if it had been a constant factor in Chinese strategy since the first millennium BC – questioning, for example, how the Mongols could have got past it in the early thirteenth century, or even doubting the veracity of Marco Polo, who arrived in China overland later in the same century, because he does not mention it. So some readers may wonder why the Great Wall does not feature in any of the battles described in this book. The answer is simply that, at most of the periods with which we are concerned at least, it was not there. We know that the Emperor Shih Huang-ti of the Ch'in dynasty built a wall, or a series of walls, along the northern frontier of China at the end of the third century BC, but we cannot be sure what sort of obstacle it was, or exactly where it ran, or whether it was even a continuous barrier. In fact the emperor's biographer Ssu-ma Ch'ien, whose account is our main source for the Ch'in era, implies that it was not continuous, referring instead to a scheme which involved the fortifying of forty-four cities, the utilisation of natural mountain barriers, and the construction of earth ramparts 'at other points where they were needed'. Some later dynasties also built fortifications – mostly of earth rather than stone – at various points along the frontier, but others, like the T'ang, placed less emphasis on defensive measures, and allowed the works of their predecessors to fall into disrepair. The Wall as we know it today was constructed under the Ming dynasty in the sixteenth and seventeenth centuries AD, and it runs far to the south of most of the earlier defensive lines – none of which are likely to have been as formidable an obstacle as the modern stone structure, even when newly built.

Another related myth portrays the Chinese as a uniquely unmilitary people, who have always preferred to rely on technology or sheer cunning to overcome their enemies, rather than brute force. This ties in neatly with the idea of an isolationist civilisation hiding behind the Great Wall, and with the emphasis on deception and psychological warfare to be found in Sun Tzu's famous classic on the *Art of War*, but as a generalisation it is highly misleading. It is true that the dominant ideology of Imperial China, as expressed in the fifth century BC by Confucius, emphasised civilian virtues in preference to military ones, and that from the seventh century AD onwards the bureaucratic elite was selected, at least in theory, for its scholarship rather than its fighting prowess. Even before the time of Confucius, rulers had often preferred to portray themselves as overawing their rivals by superior virtue rather than military might. So for example the annals of the Chou dynasty, the victor at the Battle of Mu-yueh discussed in Chapter 1, placed their emphasis on the unfitness to rule of the defeated Shang king, rather than on the innovative tactics which may in fact have been decisive on the battlefield. An often-quoted Han proverb describes a military career as a waste of talent comparable to using good quality iron to make nails. But the following chapters will show many examples of men who rose to power and fame, and even founded prestigious dynasties, by their success in war.

A more recent stereotype portrays China as the first industrial society, technologically far in advance of the rest of the world. The researches of Professor Joseph Needham and his colleagues, whose series of volumes *Science and Civilisation in China* has been largely responsible for this idea, began in the 1940s, when China was poverty stricken and politically weak, and the prevailing opinion of its civilisation in Europe was very different. It was widely held at that time that the peoples of the Far East had only ever managed to copy the inventions made in the west, and as well as being a general contribution to historical knowledge, Needham's work has been an invaluable corrective to that view. But in the absence of similar surveys for most of the rest of the world's civilisations, its very scope has tended to take things to the opposite extreme. Certainly, in the military sphere, China's undoubted technical inventiveness seems to have provided no clear advantage over enemies from outside. In fact the period which witnessed its greatest strides towards what might be called a modern industrial system, the Sung dynasty of the eleventh and twelfth centuries AD, was followed immediately by the Mongol conquests, which for the first time in history reduced the whole of China to subjection to a foreign invader.

China and its Environment

In the popular imagination, in both East and West, China is also seen as an immensely ancient civilisation, but in fact its history began rather late in comparison with many other parts of the world. The campaign which is discussed in Chapter 1 is the very first of which we have a coherent written account, and it took place at a time when the great Bronze Age civilisations of the Mediterranean, the Middle East and the Indus Valley were already in decline. And yet once established, the culture which we know as Chinese has survived, evolving but essentially uninterrupted, until the present day. Egyptians and Iraqis may take pride in the achievements of their ancient forebears, but there is little real continuity there: their countries have undergone very long periods of foreign domination in the intervening millennia, and even their language and religion are now quite different. The Greeks and the Jews may perhaps more plausibly claim cultural kinship with their ancestors living three thousand years ago, but neither have been politically independent or united for most of that time. By contrast, China has maintained its independence, its distinctive culture, and at least the ideal of unity until the present day – apart from brief periods of domination by the Mongols and Manchus, who far from destroying the native culture were quickly absorbed by it, and often became its staunchest defenders. The key both to China's late start and to its extraordinary resilience lies largely in its geography, and in order to understand the men who fought its battles, we need first to consider the world in which they lived.

A persuasive theory of the origins of what we call civilisation argues that the times and places where it arose were governed not just by chance, nor by the peculiar talents of the people involved, but by the nature of their environment. To many this sounds like an unacceptable degree of historical determinism, but it is rooted fairly solidly in basic economics. If we define a 'civilisation' as a society which is able to support an organised government, an army, a literate elite, and other non-food producing specialists, it is obvious that the first requirement is a reliable surplus of food. This depends on agriculture, which in turn requires a local supply of crops and animals suitable for domestication. In this respect the most favoured region on earth was western Asia, on the edge of what became known as the Fertile Crescent – or in modern terms roughly the area of Iraq, Syria and Israel (Diamond). Here the ancestors of domestic wheat grew wild, and herds of relatively tractable sheep, goats and cattle inspired experiments in domestication. Two of the basic components of civilisation, agriculture and settled villages, were already in evidence in this region by 8000 BC, and over the next four thousand years most parts of the Eurasian landmass which enjoyed a climate suitable for the new lifestyle were gradually occupied by settled communities dependent on these basic components. These societies were principally dominant in the coastal regions, especially in the peninsula of India, around the eastern end of the Mediterranean, and along the great rivers which flow eastwards through what is now China. Most of these regions relied on wheat or similar grains derived from Western Asia, and which were adapted to its semi-arid climate. By good fortune these conditions were also the most suitable for the domestic animals which originated from the same geographical zone, especially the horses that in the distant future were to become the most important source of military power. In the south-eastern parts of Asia, however, farmers had independently developed another grain crop, rice, that was entirely different in its requirements. Rice needs higher temperatures and more rainfall, and its cultivation is far more demanding in terms of human labour, but it is highly productive and its continued cultivation is less likely to impoverish the soil.

Thanks to its geographical location, the land which was to become China benefited, if belatedly, from both of these environments. By 6500 BC settled villages were appearing in the middle section of the Yellow River valley, in what are now Shanxi and Shaanxi Provinces, developing over the next two millennia into what archaeologists call the Yang-Shao Culture. This was a Neolithic community dependent on growing millet and raising cattle, sheep and pigs. Meanwhile in the warmer and wetter region further south, along the lower Yangtze River, people were cultivating rice. Millet, and later wheat – which was introduced to China around 1000 BC – remained the dominant crops in the north for many centuries, but by the medieval period the Yellow River region was becoming less productive as the light soil was eroded away, and today Shanxi and Shaanxi are among the poorest areas in the whole of China. By then, however, the rice-growing districts had taken over as the main food producers, thanks to transport projects like the Grand Canal which had been constructed to link the two river systems, as well as to new techniques which enabled rice to be grown in cooler and drier conditions.

So while civilisations in the Middle East declined, Chinese civilisation did not collapse but could continue to prosper.

It is believed that the dry land farming technology of the north must have derived from that of Western Asia, but the precise route by which it did so is unknown. Much of the country which lies between China and the Fertile Crescent is far less suitable for settled farming than either of those regions. On the whole the interior of Asia is too dry for growing crops, and villages could only thrive in a few locations, where the soil was irrigated by rivers or underground springs with their origins in the surrounding mountains. Elsewhere the land was either desert or grass-covered steppe, which people could only exploit by raising large herds of horses, sheep and cattle, and moving with them when necessary in search of pasture and water. Though prevented from settling in large communities and building cities, the people of Central Asia developed a range of skills necessary for their particular environment, including horse breeding and riding, iron working, and the manufacture of weapons. They were also pioneers of long-distance overland trade. In contrast to the situation in the west, the transition from the fertile coastal zone to the barren steppe is fairly abrupt in northern China, so that these wandering herdsmen were always in close contact with the world of farms and cities. They are usually depicted in Chinese writings as savages implacably opposed to Chinese culture, and the relationship between the two ways of life was often violent, but the nomads also interacted with their settled neighbours in mutually beneficial ways – for example by spreading new technologies among societies which had no direct contact with each other. As will become evident in the following chapters, Chinese warfare always owed a great deal to the methods of the steppe, however much those who adopted these methods may have despised their inventors. In fact it is possible that China's unique 'three layered' geography explains a great deal about the success of its civilisation. The soldiers who established and maintained its imperial dynasties were fed on sub-tropical rice, organised using methods developed in taming the great rivers of the north, and riding horses and carrying composite bows borrowed from the Central Asian steppe.

They were unique in at least one other respect. The immense expanse of the steppe, and the huge mountain barriers that surround the Tibetan

Plateau further south, almost completely isolated China from the rest of the civilised world. In fact, for the great majority of its inhabitants, the civilised world was China. The knowledge of agriculture may have percolated through from outside, as did a handful of later inventions like the horse-drawn chariot, but the memory of these events had long been lost by historic times. In the late fourth century BC Alexander the Great had embarked on the most extensive career of conquest in the ancient world, but his march to the River Oxus had taken him less than half way from Greece to the Yellow River plain. A few hundred years later the Roman and Han empires almost made contact, but they were thwarted by the intervening distances, and by the reluctance of the people living in between to relinquish their middleman position in the silk trade. In the eighth century AD a Chinese and an Arab army briefly clashed in Central Asia, but the Chinese were defeated – due to the treachery of their allies rather than any military incapacity – and quickly retreated behind the Pamir Mountains where the Arabs could not follow. It was not until the rise of the Mongol Empire in the thirteenth century that China and Europe even became aware that there was another civilisation at the opposite end of the Eurasian continent. So the Chinese military tradition, like most other aspects of its culture, developed largely in isolation and evolved in its own independent direction. For these reasons alone it would be worthy of study by western historians, but it is also a fascinating story in its own right, rivalling that of any other part of the world in its colourful heroes and villains, its feats of arms and its examples of military genius. It is to be hoped that the handful of examples in this book will help to establish China's rightful place in the wider history of warfare.

A Note on Chinese Names

As in my previous writings on the subject I have retained the old Wade-Giles system for transliterating the Chinese names which appear in the text. An exception has been made for modern place-names such as Beijing, which are more likely to be familiar in the Pinyin version currently approved in the People's Republic of China. Wade-Giles is still the system likely to be most commonly encountered in both popular and academic works published in the west, and although Pinyin is steadily gaining ground, its pronunciation rules are much less intuitive and accessible for English-speaking readers.

A Timeline of Imperial China

It is customary to treat the long history of pre-modern China under headings named after the imperial dynasties which held power – or aspired to it – at the time. The best known of these – Han, T'ang, Sung, Ming – are often used as a shorthand for periods which in Europe have to be designated by rather more long-winded titles: Late Antiquity, Early Medieval, etc. The system is far from perfect, as there were extensive periods during which no single dynasty ruled the whole of China, but the following list gives a chronological sequence of the main contenders, and may be helpful in placing unfamiliar events in their historical context. Regimes which received the allegiance of the whole of what was regarded at the time as being the sphere of Chinese civilisation, generally referred to as 'All Under Heaven', are shown in capital letters. Those laying claim only to a part of this territory, or whose hegemony was disputed throughout the period indicated, appear in lower case. Some of the main developments in military science appear in brackets at appropriate points.

HSIA   c. 2000 to c. 1750 BC.
SHANG   c. 1750 to c. 1027 BC.
(Introduction of the chariot and the composite bow, c. 1300 BC.)
WESTERN CHOU   c. 1027 to 771 BC.*
EASTERN CHOU   771 to 256 BC.

(Invention of the crossbow c. 500 BC. Sun Tzu's *Art of War*, c. 500 BC. Cavalry introduced 307 BC.)

The authority of the Chou kings was only nominal after 707 BC. The last ruler of the Chou royal house was deposed in 256 BC by Ch'in, which did not proclaim its own imperial dynasty until 221 BC. The era of the Eastern Chou and the following interregnum is traditionally divided into the 'Springs and Autumns' period from 771 to 480 BC, named after the 'Springs and Autumns Annals' which are the main historical source for the events of the time, and the 'Warring States' from 480 to 221 BC.

CH'IN	221 BC to 207 BC.
WESTERN HAN	202 BC to AD 9.
'Hsin' Interregnum	AD 9 to 23.
EASTERN HAN	AD 23 to 220.
The 'Three Kingdoms'	AD 221 to 285.

The 'Three Kingdoms' held power in different parts of the empire simultaneously. Wei in the north and Shu Han in the south-west were suppressed by Tsin in 265, while Wu, in the south-east, held out until 285.

TSIN	AD 265 to 316.

(Introduction of stirrups and horse armour, c. AD 300.)

'Northern and Southern Dynasties'	AD 316 to 598.

China at this time was ruled by a bewildering succession of local regimes, led mostly by 'barbarian' elites in the north, and native Chinese in the south. The Northern Dynasties, with the ethnic origins of their ruling houses, were as follows:

Former Chao (Hsiung-nu)	AD 304 to 329.
Later Chao (Chieh)	AD 319 to 350.
Former Yen (Hsien-pi)	AD 337 to 370.
Former Ch'in (Ti)	AD 351 to 394.
Northern Wei (Toba)	AD 386 to 535.
Eastern Wei (Toba)	AD 535 to 550.
Western Wei (Toba)	AD 535 to 557.
Northern Ch'i	AD 550 to 577.
Northern Chao	AD 557 to 581.

The succession in the south was:

Eastern Tsin	AD 317 to 420.
Liu Sung	AD 420 to 479.
Southern Ch'i	AD 479 to 502.

Liang	AD 502 to 557.
Ch'en	AD 557 to 589.
SUI	AD 581 to 618.
T'ANG	AD 618 to 907.
'Five Dynasties and Ten Kingdoms'	AD 907 to 959.

The 'Five Dynasties' of the north claimed to be the legitimate rulers of the whole of China, but in reality the south was divided among a collection of local warlords. The northerners were mostly of Turkish origin, and their regimes were as follows:

Later Liang	AD 907 to 923.
Later T'ang (Sha-t'o Turk)	AD 923 to 936.
Later Chin (Sha-t'o Turk)	AD 936 to 946.
Later Han (Sha-t'o Turk)	AD 946 to 951.
Later Chou	AD 951 to 959.

Controlling part of north-eastern China throughout this period was:

Liao (Khitan)	AD 907 to 1125.
(First incendiary naphtha weapons, c. AD 900.)	
NORTHERN SUNG	AD 960 to 1126.
(Incendiary gunpowder weapons and fire-lances, c. 1000.)	
Hsi Hsia (Tangut)	AD 1038 to 1227.
Chin (Jurchen)	AD 1125 to 1235.
Southern Sung	AD 1127 to 1279.
(High explosive gunpowder weapons, c. 1220.)	
YUAN (Mongol)	AD 1260 to 1368.
(First guns, c. AD 1280.)	
MING	AD 1368 to 1644.
(Appearance of rocket batteries in warfare, c. AD 1400.)	
CH'ING (Manchu)	AD 1644 to 1911.

* The first date in the Chinese annals which can be precisely matched with its counterpart in the modern calendar is generally considered to be 841 BC. All earlier dates are approximate.

Chapter One

The Verdict of Heaven: The Chou Revolt and the Battle of Mu-Yueh, 1027 BC

'His heart was malign and he was unable to fear death... Therefore Heaven sent down destruction on Yin'. The *Shu Jing* (*Book of Documents*).

The First Dynasties

After farming, the next stage in the evolution of civilisation was the appearance of organised states, possessing a form of central authority that could mobilise large numbers of people for public works projects. In many places the impetus for this is believed to have been provided by the need for flood control, which explains why the first such states tended to appear along the banks of major rivers like the Nile and the Euphrates. So in China the first signs of towns, writing, and civil and military organisation are found along the middle and lower course of the Yellow River. Flowing 3,395 miles eastwards across North China, from the Tibetan Plateau into the Yellow Sea, this is the world's seventh longest river. Its lower reaches traverse some of the most fertile and densely populated farming land on earth, in part created by the silt washed down from the mountains by the river, but further upstream it winds through the heart of the Central Asian grasslands, home of the nomadic horse-breeders. So as well as being an archetypal 'cradle of civilisation', it is also situated on what has been for millennia one of the world's most turbulent ecological frontiers, that between the rain-fed agricultural civilisations of the Eurasian littoral zone, and the pastoral nomads of the arid interior. The river itself was also a challenge to the early inhabitants of the valley through which it runs, because the erratic rainfall on the western mountains can give rise to unpredictable floods, while the same fertile silt that makes the river so attractive to farmers obstructs its flow and makes it liable to sudden and catastrophic changes of course. Hence the very earliest Chinese historical traditions tell of local headmen – anachronistically described as 'emperors' and their 'ministers' – who took on this challenge, mobilising the peasantry to divert the floodwaters into channels which were more easily controlled. Once men had become accustomed to being called up at certain seasons, and techniques had been developed for administering, supplying and commanding them, the rise of armies and the employment of military means to extend the rulers' control must have been a natural progression. All this took place long before the appearance of written records, but when China does finally emerge into history its political centre is just where this theory would predict, in the valley of the Yellow River. It is no coincidence that all of the battles described in this book, with the exception of those fought by Chinese expeditions operating beyond their own frontiers, took place in the area once occupied by the Yang-Shao Culture.

In the Chinese historical tradition the first named dynasty was the Hsia, but little is known about it except that the ruling family was overthrown by its successors, the Shang (alternatively known as Yin), early in the second millennium BC. The Battle of Ming T'iao which brought the Shang to power was said to have occurred in 1763 BC, but we have no reliable information about the events surrounding it. Nevertheless our main written source for the Shang, the Han period historian Ssu-ma Ch'ien, has been shown to be consistent with the list of kings derived from excavated inscriptions, so there is no reason to doubt the general outline of events. Archaeology suggests a great deal of continuity between the two regimes, and there is no reason to believe that the Shang were invaders coming from outside the Hsia territories. At about this time, however, bronze tools and weapons – probably originating from the Middle East via Siberia – began to replace stone and bamboo, and there is evidence that the possession of metal weapons and armour may have encouraged the rise of a military aristocracy. A few centuries later, via the same route, came further advances in weapons technology – the horse-drawn chariot, and the composite bow.

The contrast between the graves of the ordinary people and those of the nobility, who were buried with expensive goods and even with sacrificed slaves, implies that the Shang was a highly stratified society.

According to the account of the Shang kingdom which appears in the Chou period classic *Shu Ching*, or *Book of Documents*, the kings exercised direct control only over a limited area centred on the royal palaces. One of the earliest of these centres was at Erlitou, not far from the site of the later city of Lo-yang, but around 1300 BC the capital was moved to its final site at Anyang, lower down the Yellow River, where the remains of an impressive palace complex have been excavated. Beyond the royal domain were semi-independent vassal states who owed allegiance to the kings, but often fought among themselves. Further out were the 'barbarians', who were not necessarily ethnically distinct from the Shang, but who had not adopted what were considered to be the essential elements of their culture. Some of these peoples were 'allied barbarians' who supplied auxiliaries for the Shang armies, while the rest were 'wild' and hence regarded as legitimate targets for regular military expeditions. Human sacrifice seems to have been an important part of Shang ritual, and it is likely that the main purpose of warfare was the capture of prisoners as well as booty. Much of our knowledge of Shang organisation comes from excavated 'oracle bones', on which questions were inscribed to be put to the ancestors on behalf of the kings, and these reveal that aggressive war was one of their main preoccupations.

Among the peripheral groups who were subjected by the Shang early in the Anyang period was a people known as the Chou, who lived along the upper reaches of the Yellow River in what are now Shaanxi and Gansu provinces. At first the Chou may not have been as well organised as the Shang, but being on the trade routes to the west they were at least as advanced technologically. They were familiar with the use of bronze, and may have been responsible for introducing the chariot to their neighbours further east. The *Shi Ching* or *Book of Songs*, another of the classics of the Chou period, also describes their skill in the art of fortification:

> *They raised the outer gate; the outer gate soared high.*
> *They raised the inner gate; the inner gate was very strong.*
> *They raised the great earth-mound, whence excursion of war might start.*

Archaeological finds from Chou territory dating from the century after 1300 BC include bronze vessels cast in Shang styles, and collections of oracle bones which may have been produced either for visiting Shang kings or by local chiefs in imitation of Shang rites. By the eleventh century BC, however, the oracles were less common and the bronzes began to be decorated in a more distinctive local style, a move which has been interpreted as a sign of growing independence (Rawson). But if this is correct, the message seems to have been lost on the Shang.

The Revolt of the Chou

By the middle of the eleventh century BC the Chou had expanded to control the whole of the valley of the River Wei, a tributary of the upper Yellow River, in the region which was later to be known as the 'Land Within the Passes'. This was a naturally defensible stronghold protected against invasion from the east by mountains, which was to form the power base of most of the early Chinese dynasties. At around this time the ruler of the Chou, Duke Wen, introduced a number of administrative reforms which greatly strengthened the state, but he remained at least outwardly loyal to his overlord, the Shang King Shou Hsin, who had bestowed on him the title of 'Count of the West'. Shou left Wen to guard the northern and western frontiers while he went on campaign in the south-east, but on his return he became distrustful of his subordinate and had him imprisoned. The *Shu Ching* portrays Shou Hsin as a tyrant given to drunkenness and debauchery, who was unpopular even with many of his own people, but as this source was written during the reigns of Wen's descendants and was concerned with legitimising the Chou takeover, it cannot be regarded as unbiased. The theme of Shang drunkenness recurs so often in Chou texts that Jessica Rawson has suggested that alcohol may have played an important part in their religious rituals, an idea supported by the number of elaborate bronze drinking vessels that have been discovered. The Chou may have associated these rites with Shang domination, and consciously rejected them after their victory. It is likely in any case that Shou Hsin had good reason to be wary of Wen, whose realm now rivalled the Shang royal domains in extent, and – according to the Chou account at least – was now better organised.

In the event Wen's arrest provoked the disaster which it was intended to avoid, as the Chou people threw off their allegiance to the Shang and raised an army of invasion. 'Therefore', says the *Shu Ching*, 'Heaven sent down destruction on Yin.' The agents of divine vengeance were led by Wen's son Wu, who ostensibly took up arms reluctantly in order to free his father. This was one of the most significant events in the whole of Chinese history, but it is symptomatic of the poverty of our sources for the period that several widely differing dates have been ascribed to it. The *Han Shu*, or Official History of the Western Han dynasty, provides a date that corresponds to 1122 BC in the western chronology, but an apparently older text, the *Bamboo Annals*, gives a sequence which would place the revolt almost a century later, in 1027 BC. The latter remains the most widely followed version, although some modern scholars have proposed a compromise between these figures, suggesting that the fall of the Shang should be dated to around 1050.

Armies of the Shang Era

Our main source for Shang military organisation comes from the inscribed oracle bones, which indicate that the armies consisted of two grades of troops, known as 'tsu' and 'lu'. A 'tsu' was an extended family or lineage group which seems to have been one of the basic elements of society, and which apparently also functioned as a military unit in time of war. Some 'tsu' units were commanded by members of the royal family, and these may have been regaded as an elite, since they appear to have been sent on distant expeditions more frequently than other units. The 'lu' troops were often more numerous – 10,000 in one inscription, compared to 3,000 'tsu' – and may have formed a standing army under the direct control of the king. From surviving weapons discovered in tombs of the Shang dynasty, plus the occasional hint in written sources, it is also possible to build up a picture of the armament and style of fighting of the era. Yang Hong records that of the 939 tombs excavated at Anyang between 1969 and 1977, more than 160 contained weapons, which were invariably associated with male skeletons and can be presumed to represent the equipment which they used in war. Tactically the soldiers were classified as 'ma', or chariot riders, 'she', or archers, and 'shu', infantry equipped for hand-to-hand fighting. The tomb of a Shang nobleman excavated at Hsiao T'un included a contingent of bodyguards, who may have been deliberately killed to accompany him in the afterlife, and who have been taken as possible evidence for Shang small-unit organisation. The tombs were divided into five groups, each of which comprised a chariot with five associated bodies, plus another twenty-five buried without vehicles. Other chariot burials also occur in groups of five or twenty-five. This could represent a system in which chariots were organised into multiples of five, each vehicle being supported by five times that number of infantry, but it is not known how widespread this organisation may have been.

The commonest close combat weapon was the 'ko' or dagger-axe, which is associated archaeologically with both charioteers and footsoldiers. In its basic form it consisted of a transverse dagger-shaped bronze blade, usually around a foot in length, fixed to the end of a wooden handle by means of a tang inserted into a slit in the shaft. The length of the shafts is not always easy to determine as the wood is seldom preserved, but Yang Hong mentions examples varying from 60cm (which may only be a fragment of the original) to 1.4 metres. Those from one site at Anyang had originally been painted red. Some examples have an elliptical cross-section which would make them easier to grip when striking a sideways blow. The longer shafts are generally associated with spears rather than dagger-axe blades, so it is likely that the infantry version of the 'ko' at least was short enough to be wielded in one hand. In the later Shang period the blade often had a downward curving projection which was perforated so that it could be lashed to the shaft, performing the dual purpose of increasing the cutting edge, and strengthening the attachment to the handle. It is possible that the concave cutting edge was useful for slashing the reins of attacking chariots. Nevertheless the dagger-axe remained a fairly crude weapon, designed only for a sideways or downwards blow and requiring plenty of space to swing effectively. In later centuries a spear point was commonly added to the end of a longer shaft, and the 'ko' was developed into a much more effective multi-purpose cut-and-thrust weapon, similar to a medieval bill. At least one example of this type has been excavated from a Shang tomb, at Taixi in Hebei Province, which shows that the idea was known, but the great majority of Shang versions seem to have lacked the point. Separate bronze spearheads are known from several burials, but they are much rarer than the dagger blades. Bronze blades of similar dimensions, often slightly curved, were also designed with ordinary knife handles, and may have been used as tools or sidearms. Several examples of what Yang Hong calls 'dao' or single-edged swords have blades of a foot or less, and might be better described as daggers. Axes of a more conventional type, known as 'yueh', were also used, although many of the larger axe heads weigh around twenty pounds, and were surely too heavy to have been swung in combat. They tend to be elaborately decorated, and probably functioned as symbols of authority, for executing prisoners, or both.

The characteristic missile weapon of the Shang warriors, again used both on foot and by chariot riders, was the bow. Being made of organic materials these weapons do not survive in archaeological contexts, but 'kung mi' or string holders, and the bronze fittings known as 'pi', which were attached to the grip and apparently helped the unstrung bow keep its shape, are often an indication that bows were once present in a burial. Barbed bronze arrowheads of various designs have also been found. From drawings and other hints it has been deduced that the typical Chinese composite recurved bow, originally derived from Central Asia, was already in use under the Shang (Yang Hong). This would not be surprising, as archaeological finds suggest that such bows were known in Siberia as early as the third millennium BC (Karasulas). Constructed from strips of bamboo, animal horn and sinew glued together, they were the product of a long and complex production process, and so may at first have been restricted to the wealthier warriors, explaining why archery equipment is most commonly associated with chariot burials. The Shang infantry also included archers, but bows do not seem to have been buried with them as frequently as close combat weapons. The composite bow was better suited to mounted combat than the wooden self bow popular in Europe and elsewhere, because it could be made shorter for the same amount of power, and so was easier to handle in a vehicle or on horseback. Because of its recurved shape, the limbs of the bow also return to position more quickly from the draw, giving the arrow a higher initial velocity and hence a theoretically greater range. In at least one respect this imported weapon was improved by the Chinese, since they were able to replace the Central Asian animal-sinew bowstrings with silk, which was stronger for its weight, and until modern times was regarded as the best material for this purpose in both east and west. The contrast between the highly sophisticated composite bow and the rather crude dagger–axe with which it was associated is striking, and suggests that archery was regarded as the main offensive tactic, with hand-to-hand fighting perhaps considered a last resort. This is in fact a theme common throughout Chinese history, and although other weapons went in and out of favour at various times, the one constant in the Chinese armoury was always that invention of the despised Central Asian 'barbarians', the composite bow.

Yang Hong rather optimistically describes the bow and the dagger–axe as 'an integrated set of weapons', but the examples he gives of warriors being found with both weapons all refer to chariot burials. Burials containing chariots were common at the site of Anyang, but are not found at the earlier centres, a fact which suggests that the vehicles were not introduced until around 1300 BC. By that time they had been an important element in Middle Eastern armies for at least three centuries, and it is generally accepted that the Chinese versions were introduced from the west, or at least inspired by knowledge of western war chariots (Piggott 1992). It has even been suggested that the organisation of Chinese chariots in units of five may have been derived from that of the Mitanni who ruled in northern Syria around 1500 BC (Anthony 2007). This idea is supported by the discovery of rock carvings of wheeled vehicles in Mongolia, and by apparent similarities between chariot burials excavated in China and the Caucasus (Rawson). If chariots were introduced via Central Asia, it would not be surprising if the northern and western neighbours of the Shang had acquired them at the same time or earlier, and Shang inscriptions do record the capture of vehicles from enemy tribes. The Chou were famous horse breeders, and certainly possessed chariots by the time of the Mu-yueh campaign. According to the *Ssu–ma Fa*, a manual on the art of war which probably dates from the fourth century BC, they had developed their own tactical methods which placed emphasis on weight and armament rather than mobility: 'As for their war chariots... Those of the Shang were called "chariots of the new moon" for they put speed first. Those of the Chou were called "the source of weapons" for they put excellence first.' (Sawyer, 1993). The *Ssu–ma Fa* is a very late source, but it is supported by archaeological evidence, which shows that under the Chou dynasty the two-horse chariots of the Shang were replaced by heavier vehicles drawn by teams of four.

Evidence from burials suggests that Shang chariots usually carried three crewmen (Yang Hong), of whom one was presumably an unarmed driver, and this was certainly the norm in the Chou period. It is not clear whether the two fighting crew comprised a specialist archer and a man armed with a dagger-axe for protection at close range, or whether both men would normally carry both types of weapon. Chariots were probably not available in very large numbers at this date, and an inscription dated to the twelfth century BC may give us an idea of the relative proportions of charioteers and footsoldiers in most armies: 1,570 prisoners were recorded as taken in one campaign, but only two chariots – though the latter, being more mobile, might of course have been under-represented among those captured. Vehicles were no doubt expensive to manufacture, and the horse teams costly to feed, so we can assume that they were restricted to the aristocracy, an assumption which is confirmed by the extravagance of most chariot burials. Chariots did become more common in later centuries, however, and a poem preserved in the *Shi Ching* refers to a unit of 300 'bright' vehicles, all drawn by teams of matched bay horses with white bellies and black manes. Yang Hong mentions a tomb containing a man who was buried with a dagger-axe, a bow and a horse, but no chariot, which he interprets as evidence for Shang cavalry. However later Chinese tradition is adamant that riding horses in battle was regarded as a 'barbarian' practice, and was not adopted until the end of the 4th century BC. This does not preclude the appearance on Shang battlefields of occasional mounted messengers or scouts, who might perhaps have been mercenaries from beyond the frontier, but there seems to be no evidence for organised units of cavalry at this time or for many centuries afterwards.

The most common item of defensive armour in Shang tombs is the helmet, cast in solid bronze and usually ornamented with ferocious animal head designs. Yang Hong notes that the inside of the helmets was left unpolished and rough, implying that a soft lining, or perhaps a turban, must have been worn under them to protect the head. This would in any case be necessary in order to avoid concussion from heavy blows with a dagger-axe or similar weapon, and some bronze figurines of the period show what seems to be a turban worn without the helmet. Traces of what is thought to be leather body armour have also been found, as well as circular bronze plates which might have been used to reinforce a leather cuirass. Shields seem to have been made from painted leather stretched over a wooden or bamboo frame, which would have provided a flexible defence far more effective against arrows than wood alone, but could have been demolished fairly easily by repeated blows from a dagger-axe. From these clues we can deduce that Shang infantry probably did not habitually go into battle in close order, relying on overlapping shields for protection, but rather fought as individuals, in a loose formation which would have allowed room to parry with their dagger-axes or catch arrows on their shields. This may not always have been the case for the Chou, as the narrative of the battle at Mu-yueh will show, but otherwise there is no evidence that they were armed or equipped differently from their Shang counterparts.

Decision at Mu-yueh

The final battle which overthrew the Shang was one of the most decisive in China's history, as well as being the earliest of which any details have been preserved. Unfortunately, however, those details are still insufficient to give us a coherent picture of the action. The battlefield of Mu or Mu-yueh is generally identified as being in modern Henan Province, south of the Yellow River and not far south-west of the Shang capital at Anyang, which would obviously make sense if a Shang army was confronting an invader coming from the west. The site is described in the Chou sources as a 'wilderness', meaning that it was uncultivated and so perhaps partly wooded – or, being near the river, marshy. Duke Wu's army is said to have included 3,000 Chou noblemen and 800 Shang defectors, although his total force, including the lower class footsoldiers, would presumably have been much larger. The Shang forces, commanded by Shou Hsin in person, were far stronger in numbers: half a million men is traditionally quoted, but this vast number must surely be an exaggeration. Shou's army included many slaves who had been hastily armed for the defence of the capital, and our admittedly pro-Chou sources repeatedly emphasise the unpopularity of the Shang king and the low state of morale of his army.

In the Chou camp the mood was very different. Their lack of numbers seems only to have strengthened their resolve. The troops first took a mass oath of loyalty to their leader, immortalised in later accounts as the

'Pledge of Mu'. Then Wu issued his orders for the coming fight. His troops needed to concentrate on mutual support in order to counter the enemy's numerical advantage, and so, according to the account in the *Shu Ching*, they were instructed to advance at a steady pace, maintaining close formation rather than fighting as individuals. 'Do not exceed four or five strokes, six or seven thrusts' they were told, 'then halt and line up.' It is hard to imagine chariots fighting in this way, and so we can assume that Wu's battle plan depended mainly on his infantry, possibly because the ground was unsuited to vehicles. Another reason for insisting on maintaining a solid formation may of course have been to prevent the more numerous Shang chariots from breaking through, and if the Chou vehicles were indeed heavier and better armed, they may have fought in close co-operation with the infantry in order to counter their opponents' greater mobility. There is a hint in the *Shu Ching* that further defections from the Shang may have taken place during the battle itself. We are told that when the lines clashed the Shang front rank turned around and threw those behind it into disorder, although we do not know whether this was deliberate treachery, or simply a result of their inability to make headway against the close-packed Chou columns. At any rate the rest of Shou Hsin's army must have continued to stand its ground, for the battle was long and hard fought, and the less well organised Shang troops suffered terrible losses. Enough blood was spilled, the *Shu Ching* says rather imprecisely, 'to float a log'. Eventually the Shang line broke, and Shou Hsin fled back to his palace, where in his rage and despair he burned himself to death.

The Triumph of Chou

The way in which Wu exploited his victory was to set the pattern for many subsequent changes of dynasty in China. Publicly he proclaimed that Heaven had withdrawn its support from the Shang because of its rulers' vices, and had transferred the mandate to rule to the Chou royal house. Henceforth Heaven's favour was to be encouraged by careful observance of the necessary rituals, as well as by wise government in the interests of the people. The capital was moved west from Anyang to Hao, in the 'Land Within the Passes'. However, in reality many elements of the decentralised Shang political system were retained, probably because most of the local magnates who had assisted the Chou conquest were too powerful to be subjected to direct control. Four of these men were established in the 'Duchies' of Sung, Yen, Lu and Ch'i, owing nominal allegiance to the Chou king, but effectively independent. Sung, situated in what is now the province of Henan between the Yellow River and the River Huai further south, was given to Shou Hsin's heir in return for his acquiescence, but in 1019 he rebelled, in alliance with disaffected Chou nobles. The revolt was suppressed in 1017, but Wu seems to have realised the need to reward his own followers to guarantee their future loyalty, and he divided much of the region under his own control into separate fiefs, most of which went to members of his own family.

In the long term the results of this were unfortunate, because the Chou king no longer controlled his own armed forces, but was reliant on his vassals to provide troops when called upon. Despite this disadvantage Chou armies were at first generally successful, and over the next two centuries the boundaries of the empire were extended, notably in the direction of the Yangtze valley. In that remote region a rival state was gradually coalescing – Ch'u, which claimed descent fom the ancient Hsia dynasty, but which was in fact a confederation of local tribes more or less influenced by northern culture. The Chou sent numerous expeditions against Ch'u, on one of which King Chao was drowned in the Yangtze. But despite such setbacks the southerners were reduced to at least a nominal subjection to the dynasty, which at least in theory extended its rule over an area more than twice the size of the former Shang realm. Then in 771 BC disaster struck.

The Chou had long been in contact with peoples living north and west of them who were considered to be outside the Chinese cultural area, although many of them were apparently settled agriculturalists who enjoyed a similar lifestyle. These 'northern barbarians' were not yet the mounted nomads who were later to dominate the lands beyond the northern frontier, but fought mostly on foot, although we know from Chou sources than some of them possessed chariots. In 771 one of these tribes, the Jung, invaded from the west and threatened the capital at Hao. This was the occasion of the famous story of the king who was in the habit of summoning his vassals with false alarms to amuse his favourite concubine; whether for this reason or not, they failed to answer the call and the court was forced to evacuate the city, moving east to a new site at Lo-yang, lower down the Yellow River. The Jung were eventually repelled, but Lo-yang remained the seat of the Chou royal house until it was finally suppressed in 256 BC. The prestige of the dynasty was irreparably damaged, and from then on the real power in the Chou kingdom belonged to the great feudal vassals. In 707 BC King Huan made a last attempt to restore royal authority, summoning the magnates to support him against a rebellious former minister, Earl Chuang of Cheng. This time they mustered their troops as ordered, but at the Battle of Hsu-ko they deserted and left Huan to be surrounded by the rebels. The latter allowed him to escape out of respect for his royal rank, but after this humiliation he abandoned his right to call on his vassals for military service. Chou was now no more than another of the 170 or so contending states into which the kingdom had fragmented.

Chapter Two

The Fifty-Seven Years War: Ch'eng-P'u, Pi and Yen-Ling, 632 to 575 BC

'The war-chariots were well balanced, As though held from below, hung from above. Our four steeds were unswerving, Unswerving and obedient.' The *Shi Jing* (*Book of Songs*).

The 'Springs and Autumns'

The three centuries following the fall of Hao are known in Chinese tradition as the Eastern Chou, after the eastern capital at Lo-yang. An alternative designation was the 'Springs and Autumns' period, after the annals of the state of Lu which listed the events of each year under these two seasons. We are now firmly in the era of written history, and an even more informative account of events is provided by the classic known as the *Tso Chuan*, a commentary on the annals written by China's first true historian, Tso Ch'u-ming. At first sight the picture provided by these sources seems chaotic, as the little states which had arisen after the collapse of Chou authority fought, coalesced and split apart again in a succession of wars and temporary alliances. However, detailed studies of Tso Ch'u-ming's work have illuminated a number of underlying trends (Walker). Most significantly, a handful of the larger states began to develop organised systems of government, run by formal bureaucracies, and to expand their territories at the expense of their weaker neighbours. Despite the constant warfare this was a period of population increase and technological progress in China, and improved logistical backing enabled armies to remain in the field for longer periods and campaign over greater distances than previously. Expeditions were classified into two distinct types. A 'raid' or 'ch'in' was intended mainly to acquire booty, especially grain from an enemy's fields, and so was launched without warning and timed to arrive just before the crops could be harvested. A more honourable way of conducting warfare was the 'fa', or formal expedition with drums beating, usually preceded by an official declaration of war.

Politically the century between 700 and 600 BC was dominated by a power struggle between north and south. While the old Chou heartland in the Yellow River valley remained fragmented, the entire Yangtze region came under the control of a federation dominated by the state of Ch'u. The northerners continued to pay lip service to the royal status of the Chou dynasty, and to content themselves with the titles granted to their predecessors under the Chou system – in descending order of rank these were 'Kung', 'Hou', 'Po', 'Tzu', and 'Nan', often translated into English as Duke, Marquis, Earl, Viscount and Baron respectively. In Ch'u, however, as early as 704 the then ruler, Wu, had adopted the title of 'Wang' or King, a direct challenge to the pretensions of the Chou and an implied threat to the independence of all the other states.

The northern states responded by putting together a series of alliances as a deterrent to the ambitions of Ch'u. The first to organise such a pact was King Huan's nemesis Earl Chuang of Cheng, at the end of the eighth century, followed after his death by Duke Huan of Ch'i, who ruled from 685 to 643 BC. Ch'i was located in the east of China, its heartland being around the Shantung Peninsula and the massif of Mount T'ai, which provided it with a rich and naturally defensible strategic base. In fact Ch'i was sometimes known as 'the Ch'in of the east' – alluding to the old Chou stronghold 'Within the Passes' on the Wei River, which was now occupied by the emerging state of Ch'in. Duke Huan led several expeditions against Ch'u, often provoked by the attempts of the southerners to detach minor members of the alliance by force. Then after his death the Sung Duke Hsiang, the heir of the ancient Shang kings, briefly aspired to leadership of the anti-Ch'u coalition. However Sung had never shaken off the Shang legacy of decentralisation, and was not regarded as a credible military power. The other lords had little confidence in Hsiang, and boycotted the conference which he called to formalise the alliance. In 638 the Sung army tried to oppose Ch'u without the support of allies, and was decisively defeated at the Battle of the Hung River. According to the *Tso Chuan*, Hsiang had deployed his army for battle on one bank of the river while the Ch'u army was only halfway across. One of his ministers advised him to attack the enemy vanguard before the main body could cross to support it, but Hsiang refused. He insisted on waiting until the Ch'u troops were all across and drawn up in their battle formations, arguing that 'the sage does not crush the feeble, nor give the order to attack until the enemy have formed their ranks'. When the Sung soldiers finally did charge, the enemy were ready for them; Hsiang was wounded, and his army scattered in rout. The duke's misplaced chivalry became proverbial in China, and in the short term his weakened state was forced to seek security in an alliance with Ch'u.

The Armies of the 'Springs and Autumns'

The armies that took the field in the wars of the seventh century BC had not changed drastically from those that had fought at Mu-yueh nearly four hundred years earlier. Cavalry remained unknown, but chariots had increased in numbers, and were now the principal striking force. In most cases they continued to be crewed by three men, but the vehicles were now larger and heavier than their Shang predecessors, and were regularly drawn by teams of four horses. Bronze blades have occasionally been found which seem to have been attached to the ends of chariot axles; we do not read of the vehicles being deliberately driven into massed infantry like the scythed chariots of the Persians, but the blades might have helped to deter hostile skirmishers from climbing on board, or even have disabled opposing chariots if they came close enough. Both crew and horses could be armoured with tough rhinoceros hide, either in the form of scales sewn onto a cloth backing, or made into one-piece sleeveless coats like the leather 'buff coats' of seventeenth century Europe. Excavated bronze helmets tend to be less extravagantly decorated than Shang examples, perhaps because they were being produced in greater numbers and were no longer reserved solely for the aristocracy. The composite bow and bronze dagger-axe were still the main weapons of both infantrymen and charioteers, though now dagger-axes were often mounted on a longer shaft – as much as 18 feet in length – and were presumably wielded in two hands. This must have made them far more effective when used by men on foot against chariots, and we hear of several instances of infantry defeating charioteers, as in the Tsu campaign of 613 BC when rebellious peasants destroyed a force of 800 vehicles. Short bronze swords begin to make their appearance in archaeological sites of the Springs and Autumns period, but are not mentioned in written sources until around 500 BC. The nobility continued to rely mainly on archery, and the *Tso Chuan* reveals that individuals could achieve fame by the accuracy of their shooting, or by their ability to draw an exceptionally powerful bow. Later tradition records that the Western Chou had raised armies by what was known as the 'ching-t'ien' or 'well-field' system, in which the population was organised into groups of eight families living around a well, each of which had to supply one recruit. This was probably a theoretical system which might never have operated in practice in its pure form, but the Chou's successor states may have operated something like it. Duke Huan of Ch'i was said to have greatly increased his state's military potential by increasing the obligation to serve to one man from each family.

Tactically, the troops seem still to have been organised into fives and multiples of five as they had been in the Shang period. Infantry were deployed five deep, possibly with archers placed behind the dagger-axe men to shoot overhead, as is implied by a statement in the fourth century *Art of War* of Wu Chi that bows were given to the taller soldiers in a unit, while shorter men had close combat weapons. Formations known by names such as 'fish scale' or 'crane' and goose' are mentioned; what form these took is not always made clear, though it seems that the 'fish scale' involved chariots in line in the front rank, with infantry in support behind. It was usual to divide an army into three bodies, a centre and two wings, although the accounts of the battles discussed in this chapter show that variations on this plan were often employed to gain a tactical advantage.

Duke Wen

Fortunately, despite the failure of Duke Hsiang's initiative, events elsewhere had recently provided the northern alliance with a new leader of outstanding ability. Tsin was situated in a fertile plain north of the middle Yellow River, and was one of the largest and most populous of the northern states. However it had been racked by civil strife since 655 BC, as a result of a dispute over the succession to the ailing Marquis Kuei-chu. One of the Marquis' sons, Ch'ung-erh, had been accused of trying to poison him and had fled into exile, first among the Ti barbarians, and later in Ch'i. There he had been hospitably received by Duke Huan, but Ch'ung-erh's father had now died, and his companions were plotting to place him on the throne of Tsin. To that end they got him drunk and spirited him away to Ch'u, where King Ch'ing offered to back his bid for power if Ch'ung-erh would promise to reward him appropriately. Of course the young exile had little to offer, and pointed out that Ch'u was far richer than Tsin, and so even as Marquis he would be unable to repay the debt with costly goods. Therefore in return for Ch'ing's help he would agree that, if war ever broke out between Tsin and Ch'u, he would withdraw three times, a distance of thirty 'li' (or about ten miles) on each occasion, rather than fight his host. Then, he said, 'if I do not receive your commands, with my whip and my bow in my left hand and my quiver and my bow-case on my right, I will manoeuvre with Your Lordship'. A Ch'u general named Tzu-yu, who was in attendance, and whom the *Tso Chuan* describes as ignorant, stubborn and reckless, was outraged by the arrogance of this offer, which seemed to place a stateless refugee on the same footing as the king of Ch'u. He urged Ch'ing to have Ch'ung-erh executed, but according to Tso Ch'u-ming the king was impressed by the young man's character, and foresaw that he would make a great ruler. The Ch'u king was nevertheless reluctant to intervene personally in the politics of Tsin, but instead provided Ch'ung-erh with an escort and sent him on to Ch'in, whose ruler was known to have a grievance against the current Marquis of Tsin, Ch'ung-erh's brother E-wu, and was even then preparing an expedition to overthrow him.

So in 635 Ch'ung-erh returned to Tsin, escorted by a Ch'in army. It appears that E-wu's rule was not popular, because when they discovered that Ch'ung-erh was with the invaders the Tsin soldiers deserted, and their commanders had no choice but to open negotiations. The exile entered the capital at the head of a combined Ch'in and Tsin army, captured and executed E-wu, and installed himself on the throne with the title of Duke Wen. It appears that what he had seen of the Tsin army so far had not inspired much confidence, because as soon as he took power he instituted a tough training programme, culminating in what might be thought of as

a 'live exercise' against the minor state of Yuen. His reforms came just in
time, for in 632 the long-awaited hostilities broke out with Ch'u. It was
the complicated system of alliances which both sides had constructed as a
counter to the other which now made war inevitable. Duke Hsiang of Sung
had died, and his successor was planning to abandon the Ch'u alliance and
restore relations with Tsin. King Ch'ing of Ch'u learned of this and began
to mobilise against Sung, which appealed to Duke Wen for aid. Wen (the
former Ch'ung-erh) and his minister Tze-fan devised a plan which involved
marching through the territory of the neutral state of Wei to occupy Ts'ao, a
Ch'u satellite on the borders of Sung. The fate of Wei is reminiscent of that
of Belgium in 1914, overrun in a war between more powerful neighbours
in which it wished to have no part, but apart from strategic considerations
Wen had additional reasons for his brutal treatment of its ruler and its
people, who had insulted him and forced him to beg for his food during
his years of exile. Wei initially refused permission for the Tsin army to
pass, but was overwhelmed in a brief campaign, and the territories of both
Wei and Ts'ao were divided between Tsin and Sung. Wen's allies in Ch'i
and Ch'in had attempted to negotiate peace with Ch'u, but this evidence
of aggression on the part of Tsin persuaded King Ch'ing to rebuff them.
Although the account in the *Tso Chuan* is generally favourable to Tsin, it is
hard to avoid the impression that Duke Wen was deliberately provoking a
war. Possibly he had calculated that his army was unlikely to retain its edge
indefinitely. What was more, at the moment he had friendly relations with
both Ch'i and Ch'in, but a change of ruler in either state could alter their
position at any time.

The Ch'eng-p'u Campaign

The Ch'u king walked straight into the trap. During the winter of
633 BC he raised an army under the command of Tzu-yu, the same
officer who had once advised him to kill Wen, who advanced into Sung
and besieged the capital at Shang-ch'iu. Wen marched south as soon as
spring came in 632, summoning contingents from Ch'i and Ch'in to join
him. Allegedly King Ch'ing took fright at the size of the approaching
northern forces and ordered Tzu-yu to withdraw, but the general begged
for permission to fight, and was eventually allowed to do so. He raised the

siege of Shang-ch'iu and marched north to meet the enemy alliance. The advance guards of the two armies met at Ch'eng-p'u, in the territory of the occupied state of Wei. According to Tso Ch'u-ming's account in the *Tso Chuan*, Wen fell back for three days before the enemy just as he had promised King Ch'ing, despite the protests of his officers that this was not necessary as the Ch'u king was not present, and it was humiliating for a ruler to retreat before an officer of lower rank. An officer named Tze-fan, however, argued that 'It is the goodness of its cause which makes an army strong', and that it would be unwise to make Ch'u seem to be in the right. This argument may not have been as impractically chivalrous as it sounds. No doubt considerations of 'hearts and minds' were important, especially as Wen was leading an army composed of several independent-minded allies. But the Duke, whom Confucius was later to describe as 'crafty', may also have had strategic factors in mind. We are not told at what point the allied contingents arrived to join him, but they had much greater distances to travel than the Tsin army had, and it seems likely that Wen had made contact with the enemy before his full force was assembled. It would then have made sense for him to fall back north-westwards, in the direction from which the Ch'in and Ch'i contingents were expected to come, in the hope of linking up with them before he was obliged to give battle. Whatever his real reasons were, on the third day Wen finally halted and deployed his troops. He now commanded a large army including units from Tsin, Ch'in, Ch'i and Sung, although the sizes of their respective contributions are not recorded. The traditional formalities were punctiliously observed before the battle. Oracles were consulted, all of them – or at least all those that were remembered and recorded in the *Tso Chuan* – favourable to Tsin. Then an emissary came forward from the Ch'u lines to issue a challenge to Duke Wen: 'Will Your Excellency permit our warriors and yours to play a game?' The Duke replied in the same chivalrous terms: 'Since I have not received your orders not to fight, let me trouble you sir, to tell your nobles to look to their chariots and honour their lord, for I shall see you at dawn.'

Tso Ch'u-ming describes the next day's conflict at unusual length, complete with the sort of detail that tends to attach itself to events that were remembered as exceptionally momentous. The Ch'u army was said to be 100,000 strong. It had enjoyed a long run of victories and its morale was high, but of the three bodies of which it was composed, only the centre actually consisted of warriors from Ch'u itself. The left wing under Tou Yi-shan was provided by a motley collection of allied contingents, including men from the vassal states of Shen and Hsi, while the right, commanded by Tou Po, was drawn mainly from Ch'en and Ts'ai, two other allied states whose allegiance to Ch'u was uncertain. Duke Wen's forces numbered only around 50,000, with 700 chariots, but they were more cohesive, better led, and evidently contained a higher proportion of reliable troops from the Tsin homeland. The men of Ch'i and Ch'in were also respected fighters in their own right. The Tsin army was also divided into a centre, under Hsien Chen and his deputy Yu Ch'in, and two wings. The right was commanded by Hu Mao and Hu Yen, and the left by Luan Chi and Hsu Ch'eng. Duke Wen himself seems not to have fought in person, but to have watched the battle from an elevated post on the slopes of Mount You-shen, in the Tsin rear. He also detached a small force under Kang Sang to circle round the Ch'u army and lay an ambush on the route of its retreat, a move which suggests that he had a high level of confidence in his plan of battle, and intended to ensure that the enemy were not just driven back but annihilated.

Tzu-yu's failings as a commander were no doubt well known to Wen, and at the council of war before the battle Luan Chi had pointed out another factor that could be exploited. 'I have heard', he reported, '... that the forces of Ch'en and Ts'ai are weak and easily shattered'. So the best of the Tsin chariot fighters were deployed on the left, opposite the weak enemy right, driving chariots whose horses were protected by bardings made of tiger skins. The significance of the tiger skins is not explained in the sources, but they may have been intended to terrify the enemy's horses, especially if they were only roughly dressed and still retained the smell of tigers. However the two great banners belonging to Duke Wen were placed on the right flank, no doubt to give the impression that the main weight of the army was there. The battle opened with an advance by the chariots of the Tsin right, but after a brief exchange of arrows they turned and fled into a convenient dust cloud which had blown up in their rear. Tzu-yu led the pursuit in person, no doubt seeing an opportunity not only to defeat the Tsin but to capture or kill his despised enemy Wen. But the dust had been deliberately raised by another group of Tsin chariots led by Luan Chi, who were galloping across the front dragging tree branches behind them, and under its cover the Tsin centre was hurriedly wheeling to the right. With the elite chariots of Wen's own bodyguard in the lead, it smashed into the flank of the Ch'u left and drove it back in confusion. Meanwhile Luan Chi's deputy Hsu Ch'eng led the charge of the Tsin left, which easily broke through the fragile Ch'en and Ts'ai contingents facing it.

With both flanks in rout, the Ch'u centre had no choice but to withdraw. What happened to Kang Sang's ambush we are not told, but Tzu-yu's army was shattered, and a large number of prisoners must have been taken, for 1,000 captives and a hundred chariots were subsequently presented by the victorious Tsin to the Chou king in Lo-yang. Three days' supply of food was also captured in the abandoned Ch'u camp. Wen ordered the left ears of all the Ch'u dead to be cut off and taken home to be displayed in the temples of Tsin. It is noteworthy that our sources say nothing about the role of the infantry in the fighting, even though they must have constituted a large majority of both armies. It may be that compared with the aristocratic charioteers they were not considered to be worth recording in the chronicles, but it is equally likely that their contribution to the outcome was in fact minimal. They would have found it difficult to intervene in the fast-moving chariot actions on the flanks, and once their own chariots had been routed, the footsoldiers of Ch'u would have had no choice but to retreat in order to escape encirclement. What happened to the Ch'u commander himself is unclear; according to one version he was killed in the rout of the chariots of his left wing, but Tso Ch'u-ming hints that he survived the battle and may have committed suicide afterwards.

Duke Wen was rewarded for his gesture of loyalty to the Chou king with the title of 'Pa', or Protector, a purely honorific award which nevertheless recognised the hegemony that Tsin had now established in the north. He now felt secure enough to restore the independence of Wei and Ts'ao, and in an attempt to put the alliance on a more permanent footing he held a great conference at Wan, to which he invited ambassadors from Ch'i, Ch'in and Sung. From this time onwards Ch'in, which until then had been regarded as a semi-barbarous outsider among the states of north China, began to play a full part in the affairs of the Yellow River communities, a development which was to have momentous consequences in later centuries. In 628 Duke Wen at last made peace with Ch'u, but died suddenly soon afterwards, leaving Tsin at the peak of its power and prestige.

Encounter at Pi, 595 BC

Despite its defeat Ch'u did not abandon its attempts to gain a foothold in the Yellow River valley, and the power blocs led by the successors of Wen and Ch'ing continued to confront each other. The next major clash took place in 595 BC, when King Chuang of Ch'u invaded another of Tsin's satellite states, Cheng. The Tsin general Hsun Lin-fu marched to the relief of the Cheng capital, but before he reached the city news arrived that it had fallen. Hsun wanted to retreat, but his officers, led by Hsian Hu, argued that this would be seen by the other states as cowardly, and humiliating to a great power like Tsin. Clearly there were also important strategic considerations, since Tsin could only maintain its hegemony over the smaller states of north China as long as they believed that it was prepared to resist Ch'u's aggression on their behalf. Allegedly King Chuang was equally reluctant to give battle, perhaps because he stood to gain nothing further by victory, but risked losing his gains in Cheng if he was defeated. However the balance of military power had recently shifted to Ch'u's advantage, at least partly thanks to Chuang's own reforms. The southern kingdom was traditionally poorly organised, and its ranks were all too often swelled by a diverse collection of sketchily trained levies drawn mainly from unenthusiastic or undisciplined subject tribes. But the expedition of 595 was an exception. According to the *Tso Chuan* its troops had been thoroughly drilled and practised in manoeuvring in response to signals, while a spirit of initiative had been inculcated in the officer corps, so that in an emergency they knew exactly how to deploy and fight without instructions from the commander-in-chief. So Chuang allowed himself to be persuaded by his subordinates that on this occasion the Tsin army would be an easy victim, especially as Hsun Lin-fu was known to lack experience and his subordinate Hsian Hu had a reputation for recklessness.

The two armies deployed into line of battle and faced each other on Cheng soil at a place called Pi, but they remained in place for several days while their leaders conducted negotiations, both still reluctant to commit themselves irrevocably to battle. Meanwhile a few hotheads from both sides drove their chariots forward to skirmish, providing the historian Tso Ch'u-ming with a couple of anecdotes designed to illustrate the old-fashioned courtesy and wit which still characterised the noble warrior class. On one occasion three Ch'u champions in a chariot had been shooting arrows into the enemy lines, when several Tsin vehicles came out to drive them off. As the Ch'u team galloped off with the enemy in pursuit, they startled a stag which had been lying hidden in their path, and killed it with their last arrow. They then stopped and ceremonially presented the animal to their pursuers, who thanked them for the gift and let them go. Elsewhere a Tsin chariot became stuck in a bog as it tried to escape, and a Ch'u warrior stopped and hailed the crew, offering advice on how to free the wheels. One of the Tsin charioteers replied to the effect that the advice was appreciated, as the men of Ch'u had far more experience of running away than their counterparts in Tsin! But eventually this unofficial activity brought on a general engagement without orders from either commander. A group of Ch'u chariots charged out to chase off two persistent Tsin skirmishers, and the latter's comrades galloped to their rescue. This move was mistaken by a Ch'u officer for the beginnings of a full-scale advance. He ordered his own chariots forward, and soon the massed vehicles of both sides were involved in a disorganised close quarters struggle on both flanks. The battle was decided, as often happened in mounted melees, in favour of the side which could commit the last reserve. In this case it consisted of forty chariots which the Ch'u commander had managed to keep under his control. Our sources give no further details except that Ch'u won the fight, perhaps partly because its leaders were better trained to act without specific orders in this sort of situation. As at Ch'eng-p'u, the battle appears to have been decided entirely by the chariot forces. King Chuang happened to be with the left wing of his army when its opponents broke, and he remained with it when the pursuit began; thanks to this chance, it was the left wing of Ch'u armies which took precedence over the right from then on. This custom, the exact opposite of that prevailing in the west, eventually became standard throughout China. Chuang pursued the retreating Tsin northwards as far as the Yellow River, where he symbolically watered his horses, but he refused to press on further. In accordance with the conventions of the time he argued that it was wrong to kill more men than was strictly necessary, but it is also likely that he did not dare to advance further into hostile territory, especially as this would have required crossing a dangerous river, which would also have blocked his line of retreat in the event of a reverse.

The Battle of Yen-ling, 575 BC

The last of the three great battles between Tsin and Ch'u occurred twenty years later at Yen-ling, also in the state of Cheng. By this time King Chuang's reforms appear to have been forgotten, and Ch'u had reverted to its usual reliance on numbers rather than cohesion. The *Tso Chuan* tells us that the Tsin commander realised that he was outnumbered and so adopted a defensive posture behind a marsh, with the exposed sections of his front protected from attacking chariots by a ditch. The Ch'u army possessed a vehicle of a type known as a 'ch'ao-ch'e' or 'crow's nest chariot', consisting of a chariot body on large wheels and carrying a tall structure on top which could be used as a one-man observation post. The king occupied this post himself, and had to shout to an officer standing below, reporting what he saw and asking for an interpretation. But despite this ingenious device, the intelligence battle was won by a Tsin officer named Meao Fun-huang. Observing the enemy line of battle he noticed that, as was the usual practice, the more reliable Ch'u regulars were in the centre – where the boggy ground to their front would hamper their manoeuvres – while the wings extending beyond the marsh were held by allied units of doubtful fighting ability, contemptuously described by their opponents as 'wild tribes of the south'. Furthermore it was known that the officers in command of the two Ch'u wings hated each other, and so were unlikely to co-operate effectively. Therefore Meao persuaded his commander to adopt a new plan. He quickly strengthened both flanks, leaving only a small holding force in the centre. Then the Tsin chariots charged on the left and right simultaneously, crushing both enemy wings and enveloping the Ch'u centre before it had time to redeploy. The king of Ch'u was wounded by an arrow but was allowed to make his escape unmolested, just as had happened to King Huan of Chou nearly two centuries earlier. Ch'u's ambitions in the north had been thwarted for the time being, but new threats, originating in the remote frontier regions of the Chinese cultural area, were soon to preoccupy both of the contending powers.

Chapter Three

The Art of War in Action: The Battles of Kuei-Ling and Ma-Ling, 354 to 341 BC

'Know the enemy and know yourself. In a hundred battles you will never be in peril.' Sun Tzu.

The 'Warring States'

In the two and a half centuries following the Battle of Yen-ling, the vast land that we now know as China was transformed. Warfare was no longer an aristocratic game, but was waged with increasing ruthlessness as the larger states expanded at the expense of their neighbours. By the fifth century BC the rather genteel atmosphere of the 'Springs and Autumns' had given way to the aptly named era of the 'Warring States'. Despite the continuing bloodshed the population of the Yellow River valley was increasing dramatically, mainly as a result of improvements in agriculture, and at the same time the influence of its ancient culture began to be felt further south, among the indigenous peoples of the upper Yangtze valley and the south-eastern coast. Modern genetic studies suggest that writing and other elements of Chinese civilisation were not spread there by invasion or mass migration, as was once thought, but were probably introduced by small numbers of traders and political refugees, and adopted more or less willingly by the tribes of the south. In 518 BC Ch'u, which had itself once been regarded as a remote southern outpost, was suddenly attacked from the south-east by a new power: Wu. The armies of Wu were said to have been trained by a Ch'u defector, and they combined Chinese organisation and discipline with the natural ferocity attributed to their people. In 506 they invaded the Ch'u heartland, defeated its armies in five successive battles and sacked the capital, Ying, despite a desperate defence during which the

Ch'u forces are said to have resorted to stampeding elephants into the Wu lines. (This is not as implausible as it may sound; wild elephants of the Indian species were widely distributed in southern China at this time, and there is some evidence that they were occasionally caught and tamed from the Shang era onwards.) The Ch'u king was driven into exile, but later returned with the support of an expedition from Ch'in. Wu's brief career of conquest was terminated in 473 when it was overrun in its turn by Yueh, another new contender situated on the south coast, near the frontier with what is now Vietnam.

These southerners seem to have waged war with exceptional ferocity, making use of penal battalions consisting of criminals under sentence of death, who were forced to fight in order to protect their families from punishment. The *Tso Chuan* tells the famous story of how at the Battle of Tsui-le in 496 three ranks of Yueh convicts were ordered to advance and cut their own throats in front of the Wu soldiers, who stood watching this terrifying spectacle while the Yueh regulars took them unawares. This seems a rather unlikely waste of manpower, and may perhaps originate from a report of an exceptionally fierce charge by a Yueh 'suicide squad',

An archer, a swordsman and a dagger-axe wielder of the Warring States, as illustrated on a cast bronze vessel of the fifth century BC. Although little more than silhouettes, these figures can still convey valuable information about the costume and equipment of the time. Note the long robe and apparently more elaborate headdress of the archer at left, which may imply that he is from a higher social class than his comrades. He appears to be drawing an arrow from a quiver at his waist. The dagger-axe depicted here is of a rather primitive design, virtually unchanged since the Shang era. By the period of the Warring States, however, more sophisticated versions were in use, wielded in two hands and combining the cutting blade with a point suitable for thrusting.

but it suggests that the use of picked 'dare to die' detachments which was a prominent feature of later Chinese warfare may have been pioneered by the southern states.

Among the more traditional regimes, however, the art of war was also evolving. In the long run one of the most significant developments was the invention of the crossbow, attributed to a certain Ch'in Shih of Ch'u, who was said to have lived around 500 BC. In its original form this weapon was a fairly simple modification of the ordinary composite bow, and it may have evolved from the static bow-traps used by the jungle tribes of the south for hunting. The addition of a wooden stock or tiller, with a catch to hold the bowstring and a trigger mechanism to release it, meant that the weapon could be kept cocked and ready to shoot until it was required, and it also permitted the use of much more powerful bows. By placing his feet on the bow and pulling up with the combined strength of both arms and shoulders until the catch was engaged, an archer could now draw a bow of 350 pounds or more. One class of weapon mentioned in Han dynasty records had a draw weight of six 'shih', which equates to about 387 pounds (Rudolf). Weapons of this weight represent around twice the power of the heaviest bow that could be shot with a conventional draw. The relationship between bow power, arrow weight and range is a complex one, and these crossbows would not necessarily have outranged composite bows by a significant margin, but their ability to penetrate armour and shields at battle ranges was certainly greater. It is probably no coincidence that their appearance coincided with the gradual decline and ultimate disappearance of the war chariot. It is often supposed that a chariot must have been highly vulnerable to all types of missiles, since the death of one horse out of a team of four would bring it, at least temporarily, to a halt. However the horses were protected by armour and not easy to kill, while just wounding or irritating them would have little effect, because being harnessed together they were forced to maintain their formation, while the heavy vehicle rumbling behind would discourage any attempt to turn round and bolt. Evidence from medieval European battles suggests that the main way in which archers could defeat mounted troops was to annoy the horses and make them throw their riders, a trick to which charioteers were generally immune. A bolt from a heavy crossbow, on the other hand, probably was powerful enough to kill a horse outright. The main drawback of crossbows was the time required to cock them, which reduced their rate of fire from around six to perhaps two shots a minute. At first they were probably used mainly to defend city walls and other fortifications, but by the fourth century BC, when they begin to appear in accounts of battles in the open field, they were being employed en masse by units of picked shooters. Their simultaneous volleys may have done enough damage at the first encounter to avoid the need for protracted exchanges of missiles with conventional archers, and so negate the disadvantage of their slower shooting.

Nevertheless it was many years before the chariot lost its place in the line of battle, and during the sixth century, as the smaller states were swallowed up or coalesced into larger ones, the size of chariot forces continued to increase. That of Ch'i, for example, grew from around a hundred in the 720s to more than 4,000 in 500 BC. The 700 vehicles deployed by Tsin in 632 had increased to seven times that many a century later. A rather obscure passage in a work entitled *The Six Secret Teachings* gives details of several different types of chariots, all apparently with different tactical roles. Though traditionally believed to date from the Western Chou era, this is probably in its present form a work of the third or fourth centuries BC, but it may preserve a genuine tradition from a time when the chariot was still the main offensive weapons system in Chinese armies. It mentions 'Martial Protective Large "Fu-hsu" Chariots' with wheels eight feet in diameter, 'Martial Flanking Large Covered Spear and Halberd "Fu-hsu" Chariots' with five-foot wheels, and 'Great Yellow Triple-Linked Crossbow Large "Fu-hsu" Chariots'. The last two types apparently carried heavy crossbows, drawn by means of a winch, which must date them to after the introduction of the crossbow in the fifth century, while others were shock weapons, 'used to penetrate solid formations, to defeat infantry and cavalry'.

The continued dependence on an apparently obsolescent weapon may have been partly for prestige reasons, but in the absence of cavalry, which was not introduced until the very end of the fourth century, the chariots still represented the only arm capable of manoeuvring faster than a man on foot. It is unlikely that they were much quicker over long distances or in rough terrain, however, and the sources continue to mention instances of them being outmanoeuvred by lightly equipped 'barbarian' armies. Perhaps for this reason it became common for charioteers to dismount to fight, although they were not always eager to do so, believing that it was demeaning to their aristocratic status. We know that one nobleman of Tsin was beheaded in 540 BC for refusing an order to dismount. Meanwhile, by 500 BC, the emphasis in battle accounts was shifting from archery duels between charioteers to massed infantry charges. The old-fashioned dagger-axe had by now been modified by the addition of a spearhead which turned it from a crude chopping device into a true cut-and-thrust weapon, but the characteristic weapon of fifth and fourth century footsoldiers was the short sword, used in conjunction with a shield. The first recorded example of this tactic seems to have been in 520 BC, when Ch'i infantry surprised their opponents in a battle in Hua by throwing away their spears and dagger-axes and closing with their swords. It was to be sword and crossbow, rather than composite bow and dagger-axe, that decided the battles of the Warring States. Body armour was also evolving, with the appearance of flexible protection made of small metal or leather plates, or lamellae, which were held together with thongs or rivets, and usually attached to a fabric backing. In its fully developed form this style of armour is represented on the pottery figures of the Ch'in 'Terracotta Army', which will be discussed more fully in Chapter 4.

Sun Tzu, Sun Pin and the Rise of Ch'i

Ch'u eventually counter-attacked against its southern oppressors, and destroyed Yueh in 333 BC, but by this time events in the north were moving rapidly towards an equally dramatic conclusion. As the geographical extent, population and prosperity of the Chinese cultural sphere expanded, the more powerful of the 'Warring States' began to aspire to complete domination of the land that they knew as 'All Under Heaven'. This began an increasing spiral of violence in which mass armies were employed in wars of extermination against rivals on all sides, chronicled in an anonymous work known as the *Chan-kuo Ts'e*, or *Intrigues of the Warring States*. The superpowers of the new era were the peripheral states which had once been regarded as barbarians themselves. They had been able to increase their territory and manpower by incorporating newly 'civilised' frontier tribes: Ch'i in the north-east, Ch'in in the north-west, and of course Ch'u in the south. The old states of the lower Yellow River were now surrounded by enemies, and with no room to expand they began to fall one by one into the hands of stronger neighbours. The first to go was Tsin, which fragmented in the half century after its defeat by rebels at the Battle of Ching Yang in 453 into three successor states – Han, Wei and Chao, known collectively as the 'Three Tsins'. (This new state of Wei is not to be confused with Duke Wen's victim in the Ch'eng-p'u campaign, described in Chapter 2.) Wei and Han especially were surrounded by enemies, and their territories possessed long and convoluted borders which were difficult to defend. According to Wu Ch'i's *Art of War* they were war weary, and though their armies were well trained they lacked enthusiasm. But by the early fourth century BC the kings of the most powerful of these states, Wei, were making determined efforts to reunite the former Tsin territories under their own rule. King Wei of Ch'i, who came to the throne in 357, was equally determined to prevent this. (It is unfortunate for us that the king's name appears the same in English transcription as that of the state of Wei which was his most formidable enemy, but the Chinese pronunciation at the time is likely to have been quite different.)

The theory and practice of the art of war had a particularly long history in Ch'i, but in the early fourth century it had entered a period of eclipse. During the two decades preceding King Wei's accession, the armies of the state of Wei, and of the newly emerging state of Yen in the far north-east, had inflicted numerous defeats on Ch'i and regularly ravaged its richest districts at the base of the Shantung Peninsula. The conventional wisdom, recorded by Wu Ch'i, was that the government of Ch'i was corrupt and widely distrusted by its own people, so its soldiers were unreliable and disinclined to risk their lives. All this was to change thanks to a young man who was later known by the name of Sun Pin. His biography, written by the Han dynasty historian Ssu-ma Ch'ien, is our main source for the battles described in this chapter. Sun Pin was born in the region around the towns of A and Chuan, where the depredations of Wei had hit hardest, and he must have witnessed at first hand the humiliation of the Ch'i armies, and the destruction of civilian lives and property by the invaders. The Sun family was an old and illustrious one, and according to tradition young Sun Pin was a descendant of the sixth-century author of the famous treatise on the *Art of War*, Sun Wu, who is better known today simply as 'Master Sun' or Sun Tzu. 'Pin', incidentally, was not his real name but an alias which he must have been given much later; his original personal name is unknown. Perhaps he was inspired by the threat to his country to leave home on a quest to learn the secrets of military success, because Ssu-ma Ch'ien tells us that he studied under a mysterious teacher known as Kuei Ku-tzu, or 'Master of Ghost Valley', whose school was situated in a hidden valley high in the mountains. Among the other pupils at Ghost Valley who later achieved fame were the illustrious general Su Ch'in, Chang Yi, who later became Chief Minister of Ch'in, and P'ang Chuan, an officer from Wei who was apparently a contemporary and – at least at first – a friend of Sun Pin.

According to Ssu-ma Ch'ien's account, Kuei Ku-tzu recognised Sun Pin's exceptional ability, and so decided to present him with a copy of Sun Tzu's text on the *Art of War*. It seems rather more likely that young Sun would already have been acquainted with a work written by a member of his own family, and the traditional version may have confused cause and effect. Perhaps Sun Pin was such an outstanding pupil because he had already been familiar with Sun Tzu's methods from an early age. In any case he must have quickly earned a reputation which enabled him to obtain a post in the army of King Hui of the state of Wei. It was an accepted practice among the officer classes of the Warring States to take employment with foreign armies, and it does not seem to have been regarded as in any way treacherous or politically suspect. Nevertheless if Sun really was a Ch'i patriot, Wei seems an odd choice. It is of course possible that he was deliberately infiltrating the enemy's camp in order to obtain intelligence; none of the early sources even hint at this, but it would help to make subsequent events more intelligible.

At King Hui's court Sun again made the acquaintance of his old comrade, P'ang Chuan. According to Ssu-ma Ch'ien's version, P'ang quickly realised that Sun was a far more expert military strategist than he was himself. So, motivated by jealousy and concern for his own career, he had the newcomer accused of an unspecified crime and arrested. The result was that Sun was sentenced to one of several varieties of mutilation prescribed by Chinese law; he was branded on the face, and both his feet were cut off. This was a lesser penalty than castration or decapitation, but was still reserved for very serious crimes. Not only did it physically disable the victim, but it was considered a disgrace to his family, as he would not be buried with his body in the condition in which it was bequeathed to him by his ancestors. It was accompanied by banishment from the court, and the criminal was clearly expected to hide his humiliation by retiring to a life of seclusion. It was as a consequence of this punishment that the victim now became known as Sun Pin, or Sun 'the footless'.

In view of the eventual consequences of his treachery, some writers have wondered why P'ang Chuan did not simply have Sun executed. It has been suggested that he was hoping that his rival would not realise who had been responsible for his conviction, and so would continue to give P'ang the benefit of his expertise from behind the scenes (Sawyer, 1995). But it is also possible that P'ang Chuan was not entirely responsible for fabricating the charges against him out of nothing, and so did not have that degree of control over events. This is, after all, history written by the victor. In any event, Sun remained in Wei under house arrest until an ambassador from Ch'i arrived, and then managed to smuggle a message to him. This man, it is said, went to visit him, at once realised that Sun was an asset worth having, and arranged for his escape, taking him secretly back home in his own carriage. Could Sun have been in communication with the authorities in Ch'i all along, and might this have been the crime for which he had been punished? This is admittedly speculation, but it does provide a more coherent narrative than the series of coincidences invoked by Ssu-ma Ch'ien.

Once back in Ch'i, Sun joined the staff of General T'ien Chi, the supreme commander of King Wei's armed forces. The king had pursued a policy of drastic reform in civil and military matters in the hope of restoring the balance of power against King Hui's Wei, and the army of Ch'i was already growing in skill and confidence. T'ien Chi seems to have been an able officer, but like P'ang Chuan he recognised young Sun's superior talent and placed increasing trust in him. This is illustrated by the famous story of the horse race, in which T'ien won a thousand gold pieces by following Sun's advice: 'Put your slowest team of horses against their best; your best team against their middle one; and your middle team against their slowest one'. Evidently the contest involved three separate races between what were supposed to be closely matched pairs of chariot teams. By altering the running order T'ien would gain an edge in two races at the cost of decisively losing only one. Predictably he lost the race between his worst team and his opponent's best, but went on to win the next two, and thus win the match overall. He later presented his clever subordinate to King Wei, who on the strength of this simple trick is said to have immediately offered Sun the supreme command of the Ch'i armed forces. This sounds like another exaggerated story passed down in the Sun family, but if young Sun Pin had really been involved in undercover activities in Wei, the king might already have been familiar with his talents. He was in any case disqualified from actual field command by his disability, but whatever the true course of events, Sun Pin soon afterwards found himself in the position of advisor and informal chief of staff to T'ien Chi.

The Kuei-ling Campaign

In 355 BC King Hui of Wei went to war with Chao, the northernmost of the three Tsin successor states, and P'ang Chuan, now his commander-in-chief, laid siege to the Chao capital at Han-tan with an army of 80,000 men. The campaign that followed and the discussions leading up to it are described in the *Chan-kuo Ts'e*, as well as in Ssu-ma Ch'ien's biography of Sun Pin, and the opening chapter of Sun Pin's own work on the *Art of War*. It seems that one of the causes of the war was Chao's attempt to neutralise its stronger rival by concluding an alliance with Ch'i, and so Sun Pin's new employer King Wei felt obliged to intervene. However he was reluctant to commit himself fully, partly owing to fear of the Wei armies, and partly because he did not want to encourage the rise of Chao as another potential rival. Therefore all that happened was that a small Ch'i detachment, together with contingents from the minor allied states of Wey and Sung, was sent to besiege the Wei border town of Hsiang-ling. The stalemate continued for a year, until King Wei learned that armies from Ch'in and Ch'u were also advancing against the state of Wei on other fronts. Now was the time to strike.

According to Ssu-ma Ch'ien the king wanted to place Sun Pin in command of the 80,000 strong army, but Sun refused on the well-rehearsed grounds that as a convicted criminal he was not fit for the post. Instead he remained in an advisory role, with T'ien Chi as commanding general. By then Han-tan was obviously about to fall, but Sun argued that they should not march to its relief, because that would bring them into conflict with the main Wei army. He proposed instead to mount a diversion by threatening the city of P'ing-ling, in the south of Wei. On the face of it this made no sense. P'ing-ling was strongly held, and the route to the town was commanded by a regional headquarters of the Wei army around the towns of Huang and Ch'uan, where many enemy infantry and chariots were known to be quartered. What was worse, an advance in that direction would leave the Ch'i supply lines vulnerable. T'ien Chi pointed out these difficulties, but Sun urged his commander to trust him. 'We are going to make it seem' he explained, 'as though we have no sense in military matters'. So when the army approached the P'ing-ling region he told T'ien to select two of his most inept subordinates and place them in charge of separate detachments. The commanders of units from Ch'i-ch'eng and Kao-t'ang were selected for this dubious honour, and sent forward with their men to attack the town. As they marched recklessly forward, the Wei troops based at Huang and Ch'uan converged on their rear, and both detachments were surrounded and annihilated.

Then Sun Pin again split his forces, and sent a lightly equipped force of chariots towards the Wei capital at Ta-liang. He could hardly expect to capture a strongly defended city with chariots alone, though no doubt they were sufficient to alarm the country and threaten the supply routes to P'ang Chuan in the north. We can imagine that the latter had followed the progress of the Ch'i armies so far with amusement. He presumably did not know that his old acquaintance Sun Pin was controlling their strategy, and must have assumed that these feeble probing attacks were all that they were capable of. The fiasco at P'ing-ling had shown that they were not only numerically weak, but also badly led. By now it appears that Han-tan had been taken, so P'ang decided to take the opportunity to destroy the insolent Ch'i raiders. Leaving behind his baggage train and his heavy equipment, he led his men on a forced march back towards Ta-liang. But Sun Pin knew his opponent all too well. The road south from Han-tan ran near to the border of Ch'i at a place called Kuei-ling, which Sun seems to have already reconnoitred as a possible ambush site. He and

T'ien Chi force-marched their main army towards the same location, and reached it several days before the enemy arrived.

They constructed a fortified position blocking the road, probably made from unlimbered chariots with shields along the top, and a ditch in front covered by spiked obstacles to injure the hooves of the Wei horses, as prescribed in Sun Pin's own manual. Spearmen and halberdiers lined the defences, with swordsmen behind them in support, and crossbowmen deployed in the rear with orders to shoot over the heads of the men in the front ranks when the enemy charged. Pickets were placed five 'li' (nearly two miles) in front of the position to give warning of an attack. But when P'ang Chuan arrived on the scene his troops were exhausted and in disorder, straggling back along the road for miles as the less fit among them struggled to keep up. He halted and may have attempted to deploy, but Sun Pin, on seeing the state of the Wei army, decided not to wait. He ordered his men to leave their defences and charge, which they did enthusiastically, sweeping the enemy away in rout at the first onslaught. The victory was decisive, and Wei was forced to abandon the war. In his *Art of War* Sun Pin claimed to have captured P'ang Chuan, but if this was the case he was apparently cheated of the revenge he surely hoped for, because according to Ssu-ma Ch'ien the two adversaries were to meet again in battle thirteen years later. It seems possible that P'ang was exchanged as part of the peace negotiations, although it has also been suggested that Ssu-ma Ch'ien is wrong in placing him at the Battle of Ma-ling in 341, and that his capture at Kuei-ling marked, as we might have expected, the end of his career.

Ambush at Ma-ling

The years following their victory at Kuei-ling seem to have been turbulent ones for T'ien Chi and his trusted advisor. Ssu-ma Ch'ien alleges that T'ien was driven into exile as a result of the intrigues of a rival at court, the Marquis of Ch'eng, who made false allegations about him to King Wei. The *Chan-kuo Ts'e* describes how Sun Pin tried to persuade T'ien to use his troops to mount a coup and overthrow the Marquis, but that T'ien refused to do so. Instead he and Sun fled to Ch'u, and watched in frustration from the sidelines as the Ch'i armies were led to defeat by less inspired commanders in two wars against Ch'in and Chao. Then when King Wei died in 343, his successor, Hsuan, recalled the exiles and once again placed his armies under their joint control. By this time the reputation of the Ch'i soldiers, at least when led by Sun Pin, stood far higher than it once had. In the *Chan-kuo Ts'e* they are described as eating human flesh and cooking the bones (or in an alternative translation using the bones as fuel for their fires), without being driven to think of mutiny. This cryptic comment might be a metaphor for their ferocity in battle, or it might be intended to illustrate the depths of hardship which they were prepared to endure under a leader whom they trusted to bring them victory.

In Ssu-ma Ch'ien's account the events of 341 BC closely paralleled those of the Kuei-ling campaign. On this occasion Wei had joined forces with Chao to invade the state of Han, which had in its turn begged Ch'i for assistance. King Hsuan had decided to let his rivals weaken each other before he intervened, so Han was left to fight alone until its forces had lost five battles, and were close to collapse. Then the old team of T'ien Chi and Sun Pin were allowed to set their army in motion once again. They marched through western Ch'i straight towards Ta-liang, and the main Wei army came hurriedly back from Han to intercept them. Somehow the two adversaries missed each other, and T'ien and Sun slipped past to the west, with the enemy wheeling after them in pursuit. The Wei commanders are named as P'ang Chuan and Crown Prince Shen, and it is possible that their arrangements were similar to those of Ch'i, with the young prince in nominal command and the lower ranking but more experienced P'ang serving under him as chief of staff and military advisor. If so, P'ang Chuan had apparently learned nothing from his previous setback. Sun informed T'ien Chi that the people of the 'Three Tsins', Han, Wei and Chao, still regarded the men of Ch'i as cowards, and so he proposed a plan to take advantage of their prejudice. On three successive nights as they closed in on Ta-liang, the Ch'i troops lit ever diminishing numbers of cooking fires: 100,000 on the first night, then 50,000 and finally 30,000 on the third. They were now well within Wei territory, and the local people and his own patrols quickly reported this to P'ang Chuan.

The news confirmed P'ang's low opinion of the Ch'i soldiers' morale, and he concluded that after only three days inside Wei territory, more than half of them had deserted. Therefore he left most of his infantry behind under the command of the Crown Prince and pressed ahead with a picked force of lightly armed men, marching day and night, in the hope of capturing the Ch'i commanders before they realised their peril and retreated. Sun Pin had made careful calculations of his enemy's route and speed, and determined that they would reach a spot near Ma-ling soon after nightfall. Here the road passed through a narrow defile, with numerous gullies and ravines on either side where ambushers could be concealed. The Ch'i troops felled a large tree across the road, and Sun painted on it in large white letters the message, 'P'ang Chuan died under this tree'. Then he deployed 10,000 crossbowmen in hidden positions on both sides of the road, with orders to shoot as soon as they saw a torch lit.

At this point it becomes necessary to address a problem that besets every discussion of military operations in ancient China. The figures given in the sources for the size of armies are routinely far too high to be plausible on logistical grounds, but the difficulty here is rather different. A force of 10,000 men is not too large to have been recruited from the population available, nor to have been supplied or commanded in the field. But how could it have been deployed in the situation described here? A crossbow requires more space than an ordinary bow both for cocking and for shooting, since it is held horizontally rather than vertically, so it cannot be used effectively in very close order. It can be shot on a high trajectory over the heads of men in front, but even if they were drawn up ten deep, 10,000 crossbowmen could hardly have occupied a frontage of less than a mile. At Ma-ling they were in concealed positions, no doubt making use of tree trunks and other cover, and must have taken up even more space, so a force of this size could not have been positioned where they could all see a single light, nor could they possibly have been able to discharge a volley simultaneously. One solution to this sort of difficulty is to dismiss all the figures in the sources as wild exaggerations, but it is clear that reasonably accurate strength returns must have been available to commanders when planning their campaigns. Sun Tzu, for example, calculates the cost of provisions, equipment and other expenses for an expedition of 100,000 men at a fairly precise 1,000 pieces of money per day. On the other hand it seems to have been customary to state any large number in units of ten or a hundred thousand, and the chroniclers were probably in the habit of using these figures to denote units of approximately that nominal strength. One entry in the Official History of the Han dynasty implies as much when it states that the men collected for one campaign against the Hsiung-nu numbered more than 40,000, 'and were called a hundred thousand'. This may have been done simply for administrative convenience or to denote the appropriate level of command, in the same way as we might refer to a brigade or a division, regardless of whether or not it is actually at full strength. The corrupt practice of commanders inflating the numbers on the rolls in order to siphon off surplus pay and rations, which is known to have been a major problem under later dynasties, may also have been a factor. It may be best to consider the figures given in narrative sources as useful for relative strengths but not for absolute ones, or if we insist of hazarding a guess at the latter, the ratio of forty to a hundred indicated in the passage quoted above may be at least a rough guide.

So perhaps the best we can do is to conclude that waiting in ambush for P'ang Chuan was a force of crossbowmen numbering a thousand or more, of whom a significant number were in a position to concentrate their fire on the head of the enemy column. When P'ang reached the obstacle in the road he immediately sent for a torch so that he could read the message written on it, triggering a storm of bolts from the darkness that threw his troops into confusion. Perhaps not many of the missiles actually struck their targets, but even those that missed completely would have added to the unnerving sound that a volley of even a few dozen arrows can produce. Having discharged all their crossbows simultaneously the ambushers were temporarily helpless until they could reload, but their opponents of course did not know this. As the Wei soldiers fled back along the road in panic, P'ang cut his own throat to avoid capture, exclaiming 'So I have contributed to the fame of that wretch!' Sun's men then charged, scattering the Wei advance guard beyond recall. Their main body, which was following some way behind, was thrown into confusion by the fugitives and also broke in rout. Most of them no doubt made their escape, but Crown Prince Shen was taken prisoner and escorted back to Ch'i in triumph. 'Because of this', Ssu-ma Ch'ien concludes, 'Sun Pin's name became illustrious, and the *Art of Warfare* was known in the world'.

This is the version of the story related by Sun Pin's biographer, but there are obvious difficulties with accepting it at face value. Sun's stratagem relied heavily on his judgement of his opponent's character, and his ability to predict what he would do in any particular situation. This is in accordance with Sun Tzu's well known advice: 'Know the enemy and know yourself, and in a hundred battles you will be victorious'. In a period in which the military leadership of all the contending states was supplied by the same international class of aristocrats, who regularly moved from the service of one state to that of another, and many of whom were trained in the same schools and knew each other personally, this intimate knowledge of the enemy's psychology was probably not unusual. But is it plausible that P'ang Chuan was so stupid as to fall for what was essentially the same trick twice? Lau and Ames argue that in placing him at the Battle of Ma-ling as well as at Kuei-ling Ssu-ma Ch'ien had misinterpreted his sources, and that it is more likely that Prince Shen – whom the *Chan-kuo Ts'e* portrays as an inexperienced and incompetent general – was in sole command of the Wei army of 341. It would therefore have been an unknown officer of the advance guard who committed suicide on the battlefield – supposing this part of the story to have been anything more than a later invention. In Chapter Four of his *Art of War* Sun Pin introduces a discussion of the use of narrow defiles for ambushes with the remark that 'this was the tactic we used in defeating P'ang Chuan and capturing Crown Prince Shen'. But of course this does not preclude the possibility that he was referring to two different battles. This interpretation also removes the difficulty of having to explain why P'ang Chuan was allowed to return to Wei after his capture at Kuei-ling; there is no other contemporary evidence for his survival after 354, and it seems more reasonable to suppose that Sun had obtained his revenge for his enemy's treachery at that time by having him executed. In a sense, though, it would be a pity to abandon the traditional story, since the vicious and irredeemably stupid P'ang is the perfect foil for Sun Pin, and as much an icon of the Chinese art of war as the men whose genius has defined it.

Sun Pin's own subsequent fate is also unknown. His *Art of War* contains references to battles that may have taken place as late as 301, and also discusses the role of mounted troops, which are believed to have been introduced into China by the King of Chao in 307, but these passages may have been added by a later editor. Liu Hsiang, a writer from the Han era, identifies the 'Lord of Lin Wu' who appears in the third century classic *Hsun Tzu* as Sun Pin, but by that time he would have been around a hundred years old. At any rate the supremacy of the state which he served did not long outlive him. Ch'i followed up its victory over Wei by establishing a local hegemony in the north-east, but this was unexpectedly shattered in 285 BC when war broke out with Yen. The Ch'i armies suffered a catastrophic defeat, and the invaders overran the whole country apart from the city of Chi Mo. From there a relative of T'ien Chi, T'ien Tan, organised a campaign of liberation which eventually drove out the Yen occupiers. The method he used to break the siege of Chi Mo was a classic piece of deception in the tradition of Sun Tzu and Sun Pin: he persuaded the richest of the citizens to send a letter to the enemy general offering to betray the city and hand over a large amount of gold, in return for a safe conduct for them and their womenfolk. He is also said to have sent double agents to suggest that the besiegers should try to terrify the remaining hardliners inside Chi Mo by desecrating the tombs of their ancestors outside the walls. In fact, as he well knew, this would only enrage the defenders and make them eager for revenge. Then when the Yen troops dropped their guard, expecting a bloodless victory, T'ien led a sudden sortie and destroyed them. But by then the political situation in China had changed drastically. The Warring States era was coming to its bloody conclusion with the inexorable rise of Ch'in.

Chapter Four

Rivals for a Throne: Liu Pang, Hsiang Yu and the Battle of Kai-Hsia, 202 BC

'With the sword one opposes a single individual, so it is not worth studying. I will study to oppose ten thousand men!' Hsiang Yu.

The Rise and Fall of Ch'in

It was Ch'in that eventually overcame all the other Warring States, and in 221 BC set up China's first true imperial dynasty under Ch'in Shih Huang-ti – the famous 'First Emperor'. In fact from an early date the people of Ch'in had been known as exceptionally warlike. They were also numerous, strategically secure in their 'Land Within the Passes', hidden behind the mountain ranges on the Wei River, and after the reforms instituted by Lord Shang in the mid-4th century BC they were also highly organised. The late fourth century BC saw the beginning of a remarkable series of aggressive wars, as a result of which Ch'in rose from being a despised frontier region to the master of the entire empire. In 317 BC its armies defeated an allied expedition drawn from Han, Wei and Chao, killing 80,000 men. Then in 316 the states of Shu and Pa on the upper Yangtze were forcibly incorporated into the Ch'in realm, and from their newly acquired bases on the upper reaches of the great river the Ch'in armies began a series of attacks on Ch'u, further downstream. Not for the last time the flow of China's rivers became a vital strategic factor, because Ch'in raiding parties could float down the Yangtze as far as the Ch'u capital at Ying in only five days, bypassing the armies deployed along the banks and striking before reserves could be mustered to stop them. Ying was not sacked until 278, and Ch'u, a vast and populous realm in its own right, was not to be finally conquered for another fifty-five years. But Ch'in was now powerful enough to fight on several fronts almost simultaneously. A Ch'u army suffered a major defeat by the Ch'in in 312, and meanwhile the ancient states of the north, which were all too often still short-sightedly embroiled in their own rivalries, were picked off one by one. On the battlefield Ch'in troops were dreaded for their berserk charges, throwing off their armour and rushing forward 'helmetless and barefoot, brandishing their halberds', in the words of the *Chan-kuo Ts'e*. This recklessness was encouraged by the system of promotion instituted by Lord Shang, which rather than encouraging tactical skill or leadership qualities, simply rewarded men for the number of enemy heads they cut off.

The campaigns against the 'Three Tsins' in particular were conducted with extreme ruthlessness. The state of Chao was situated on the northern frontier of China, on the edge of the steppe, and not surprisingly was the first to institute regular cavalry units. Tradition has it that this advance was made in 307 BC by King Wu Ling, and for most of the following century the Chao armies relied more heavily than any of their rivals on mounted archers. This development was not enough to prevent them suffering a series of defeats at the hands of Ch'in, however. At Ch'ang-p'ing in 260, a Chao army found itself surrounded and surrendered on terms, but was massacred regardless by men eager for their quota of heads, concluding a war in which the total Chao losses were reported by Ssu-ma Ch'ien as a staggering, if clearly exaggerated, 450,000. Although irrecoverably weakened, the Chao state survived until 228, when it was overrun in another Ch'in invasion. The Ch'in conquests gathered further momentum after 238 BC, when the youthful King Cheng overthrew the regent Lu Pu-wei, who had ruled for the previous nine years, and took power for himself. Han, the bitter rival of Wei, was a relatively small state best known for its excellent iron armour and weapons. According to Su Ch'in, 'the most powerful bows and the staunchest crossbows in the world come from Han'. He also praised their swords and halberds, which 'can cleave the strongest armour, shields, leather boots and helmets'. Nevertheless they could not prevail against Ch'in's numbers and ferocity, and Han lost its fight for survival in 230. Five years later it was the turn of Wei, which had once been the most powerful state in central China. Its aggressive policies had made it very unpopular with its neighbours, and it had ended up having to fight a series of wars on four fronts, during which its strength and territory were gradually whittled away, leaving it easy prey for Ch'in. It survived into the late third century BC thanks to a regime that emphasised strict social order and the systematic study of strategy and tactics, and to the support of mercenary Hu tribesmen from the north, who fought mostly as light cavalry. Almost unnoticed in the spiral of violence, in 256 another Ch'in army had marched into the rump of the old kingdom of Chou, finally suppressing the dynasty that had nominally ruled China since 1027 BC.

Ch'u fell in 223, finally forced into surrender after the capture of its king in a battle on the Yangtze. The military writer Hsun Tzu claimed that Ch'u was defeated by Ch'in because, although it did not lack good military equipment, its soldiers did not know how to use it. This view, though, probably reflects obsolete northern prejudices, because according to Ssuma Ch'ien, writing of the civil wars after the fall of the Ch'in, the Ch'u warriors were regarded as being worth ten of anyone else's. Now only Ch'i remained to dispute King Cheng's control of the whole of China, but the state which had once produced military geniuses like Sun Pin and T'ien Tan had never fully recovered from the destructive Yen occupation, and put up little resistance to the final takeover in 221. The empire was united for the first time in five centuries, but the new Ch'in dynasty, of which Cheng proclaimed himself Shih Huang-ti, or 'First Emperor', was a very different entity from the revered but ineffective Chou. For one thing, the 'empire' now covered a much larger area, extending north into the Mongolian steppe, and beyond the Yangtze into the regions once controlled by Wu and Yueh along the south-east coast. Based on figures from Han censuses, the population of this vast territory may already have been as high as fifty million. Furthermore, this was a highly centralised totalitarian state, ruled not by its traditional local aristocracies, but by a military and civil bureaucracy appointed by the emperor and reporting to the capital at Hsien-yang. Measures such as the notorious 'burning of the books' were intended to rewrite history, removing all records of the states that preceded the Ch'in takeover, and of the compassionate philosophies of sages like Confucius whom the rulers of Ch'in so despised. The old ruling families were deported en masse to the capital at Hsien-yang in a deliberate attempt to deprive any local resistance movements of their leaders, while detachments of Ch'in troops were stationed like an army of occupation in each of the formerly independent states. Lord Shang's ferocious system of rewards and punishments was imposed throughout the empire, and gigantic construction projects like the Great Wall were carried out by hundreds of thousands of forced labourers, often at a terrible cost in lives. It must have seemed, in fact, as though the whole population of China had been reduced to servitude; one commentator recalled how mutilated victims of the Ch'in penal code were to be seen everywhere, while men wearing the red uniform of convicts 'filled half the road'.

Naturally this brutal regime was widely unpopular, and when Shih Huang-ti died in 210 his empire began to disintegrate almost at once. Two of his ministers, Li Ssu and Chao Kao, plotted to conceal the emperor's death until they had disposed of their main potential rivals, Crown Prince Fu-su and the eminent general Meng T'ien. Then they attempted to rule through their own protege, the ineffectual Prince Hu-hai. But while the conspirators concentrated on enriching themselves, rebels in the provinces began to attack the small and isolated Ch'in garrisons and seize their weapons in preparation for a general uprising. The first open rebellion came in 209 BC in Ch'u, where a man named Chen She was put in charge of a contingent of 900 forced labourers summoned to work on a building project in Hsien-yang. Heavy rain and flooding along the route delayed their arrival, and Chen, who knew that the penalty for any failure would probably be death, released the workers and encouraged them to kill their Ch'in escort. Then they fled to the mountains, and raised the banner of revolt under the slogan 'Great Ch'u shall rise again!'

The Armies of the Succession Wars

Our knowledge of the wars which followed the collapse of Ch'in authority is derived mainly from the biographies of the main protagonists written by Ssu-ma Ch'ien. He seldom gives precise details of military hardware or tactics, but it is clear from his narrative that the cavalry was now the most prominent arm in Chinese armies, if not necessarily the strongest numerically. Less than a hundred years after its introduction, and in the face of considerable prejudice against such a 'barbarian' innovation, cavalry had replaced the declining chariot arm as the principal mobile force, not just in the north but throughout the empire. In fact the best mounted fighters in the campaigns of 210 to 202 BC seem to have been southerners from Ch'u. Also evident from Ssu-ma Ch'ien's narrative is the increasing reliance on hand-to-hand weapons, especially swords. The short bronze blades of the Warring States had by now been replaced by much longer weapons, up to three and a half feet in length, which could be used effectively from horseback as well as on foot, and may in fact have been primarily designed as cavalry weapons. The historian relates how on one occasion the future First Emperor, when king of Ch'in, was nearly killed by an assassin with a dagger because the king's sword was so long that he did not have room to draw it. Bronze was now being replaced by iron, but excavated examples show that high-quality bronze swords were still in use.

One almost contemporary source which can also shed light on the armies of the period is of course the 'Terracotta Army', which was buried near the tomb of Shih Huang-ti and not rediscovered until the 1970s. The formations in which the life-sized pottery figures were buried suggest that most Ch'in troops fought on foot in close order, wearing lamellar armour made of small plates which might have been leather, bronze or iron, and carrying two-handed spears or halberds as well as swords. They were supported by archers and crossbowmen, some of whom also wore armour, but who seem to have deployed as skirmishers in more open formations, rather than shooting overhead from a rear rank. Most of the weapons are missing and the figures do not wear helmets or carry shields, although these are known from written and artistic sources to have existed. The site was partially plundered soon after it was finished, however, and if the figures had been provided with real weapons, shields or helmets these would have been valuable booty for the robbers. Other models depict armoured cavalry, who might also have been equipped with either close combat or missile weapons, and a small number of chariots, which were now probably used mainly as command vehicles. The terracotta warriors appear to represent a guard unit, buried to protect the emperor in the next world in place of the real human sacrifices which had once accompanied his Shang predecessors, and the Ch'in army no doubt included other troops who are not represented, for example the light mounted archers who had formed the first Chinese cavalry units. It is also likely that the equipment shown, rather than being specific to the Ch'in, was typical of all third century armies and their successors well into the following Han period. In fact several Han dynasty tombs contain smaller models depicted in virtually identical styles of armour. We are therefore surely justified in assuming that the men who fought at Kai-hsia in 202 BC closely resembled the figures from the Terracotta Army.

Hsiang Yu

Chen She's career was to prove short-lived. He captured the city of Ch'en without meeting serious opposition, but then made the mistake of trying to invade the Ch'in heartland 'within the passes' with his motley collection of poorly-armed followers. He was opposed by the Ch'in general Chang Han, whose own force was not much better equipped, consisting of hastily armed labourers who had been taken from the site of the First Emperor's mausoleum. Nevertheless Chang drove the rebels off and retook Ch'en. Chen She escaped, but was murdered by one of his own men soon afterwards. By this time, however, similar rebel movements had already sprung up all over the empire, and factions in Ch'i, Chao, Wei and other former states had proclaimed their independence. Most of the troops loyal to the Ch'in dynasty were still scattered around the country in small garrison towns, and in desperation the authorities turned to the once despised local nobility for help. Among these was a member of a distinguished military family from Ch'u named Hsiang Liang. Hsiang was a descendant of Hsiang Yen, a general of the old Ch'u state who had been forced to commit suicide after the Ch'in conquest, so he had no obvious reason to support the occupiers, and in fact was already secretly training local youths in fighting methods for his own purposes. Nevertheless the Ch'in governor T'ong seems to have trusted him, for when Chen She's revolt broke out he summoned him and his nephew Hsiang Yu to a conference to discuss raising troops to fight for the dynasty.

Ssu-ma Ch'ien takes up the story in his biography of Hsiang Yu. At a sign from his uncle, Yu drew his sword and cut off T'ong's head, then allegedly held off the Ch'in guards single-handed, killing almost a hundred of them, while Liang seized the governor's seals of office. The surviving government personnel were too terrified by the sudden coup to offer resistance, and soon Hsiang Liang found himself at the head of an army of 8,000 local men, all eager to join the fight against Ch'in. At first he offered his allegiance to Chen She, but when Chen was killed Hsiang decided to pursue a policy of independence for Ch'u. He located a grandson of the former Ch'u king who had survived the Ch'in purges, and placed him on the throne under the name of Huai. By this time other rebel armies from various parts of Ch'u were gravitating towards Hsiang Liang, attracted by his famous name as well as his own reputation as a leader. Among these were 20,000 men raised by a relative of Chen She named Chen Ying. With these reinforcements Liang fought several successful engagements against the Ch'in under Chang Han, but was eventually defeated and killed at the Battle of Ting-t'ao. However Chang was unable to exploit his victory and eliminate resistance in Ch'u, because another rebel army from Chao was in the field north of the Yellow River, obliging him to march off northwards to confront it. At this point King Huai showed an unexpected independent streak, regrouping the Ch'u armies and appointing new generals. In overall command he placed an officer named Sung I, with Liang's nephew Hsiang Yu as his deputy.

Apart from his role in the coup against Governor T'ong, Hsiang Yu's career up to that point had been undistinguished. Ssu-ma Ch'ien tells how he had been a headstrong and impatient youth who had tried his uncle's patience by his failure to apply himself to his studies. He had taken up writing, swordsmanship and military tactics in turn, but had abandoned them all after a short time, though he clearly had considerable ability as a sword fighter. When the war against Ch'in broke out he had been sent on a couple of expeditions against isolated towns, whose inhabitants he had casually massacred, but his only major success had been the defeat of Li You at the Battle of Yung-ch'iu, where he had fought in alliance with another rebel, Liu Pang, who had liberated his home town of Pei and styled himself its governor. Early in 207 BC Sung I and Hsiang Yu marched north with the main Ch'u army to the Yellow River, where the main Ch'in forces under Chang Han, Wang Li and Shi Chien, were besieging the Chao rebels in the town of Chu-lu on the north bank. Ch'u was not the only one of the resurgent states to march to Chao's aid, but it appears that none of them were prepared to face the Ch'in soldiers in open battle. Instead they established themselves in ten fortified camps dotted across the plain and awaited events. In view of the importance of fortified camps in this campaign and the ones that followed, the T'ang scholar Tu Mu's remarks on fortification in his commentary on Sun Tzu's *Art of War* are of interest. Although written in the ninth century AD, they describe a longstanding tradition of building elaborate defences in the field, and help to explain why commanders usually preferred to blockade an entrenched opponent rather than risk an assault. Within the outer perimeter, which was defended by an earth wall and ditch, each unit of the army would construct its own smaller fort surrounding the commander's headquarters. These forts would be sited within a hundred and fifty paces of each other so that archers and crossbowmen within could provide mutual support, with the roads between them left open, providing both fields of fire and open spaces where parades could be held. At each road intersection a small watchtower was built, on top of which was a pile of firewood guarded by a sentry, whose duty it was to light the bonfire if he heard the alarm given at night. Therefore if an enemy stormed the outer wall by night he would find himself surrounded by further fortifications, illuminated by the fires and caught in a crossfire from several positions at once. Tu Mu concludes by saying that 'our only worry is that the enemy will not attack at night, for if he does he is certain to be defeated'.

Sung I was as reluctant as his allies to attack the formidable Ch'in army, and for forty-six days he waited at Anyang, on the south bank of the river, while he dragged out negotiations with his allies. His hope was that Ch'in and Chao would fight each other to a standstill, and that even if Ch'in won, it would be so weakened by its Pyrrhic victory that it would then fall easy prey to the armies of Ch'u. Hsiang Yu, however, repeatedly argued against this strategy. He felt that if Chu-lu fell it would only strengthen Ch'in, whereas if they attacked while the Chao troops were still capable of fighting, the garrison would be able to make a sortie at the same time and trap the besiegers between two opponents. Sung I dismissed his opinion, even though the weather had turned cold and provisions were running short, so that the rank and file of the army were becoming equally disillusioned with the waiting policy. He was even tactless enough to organise a drinking party for his high-ranking cronies while the rest of the troops starved. Hsiang Yu decided that the time had come for drastic action. Entering the commander-in-chief's tent with the excuse of making an urgent report, he beheaded him with his sword, then emerged to claim that he had done so on secret orders from King Huai, as Sung I had been plotting with his friends in Ch'i to overthrow the state. It is unlikely that he really had received such orders, but no one appears to have questioned him. No doubt all ranks were happy to be rid of a commander whose conduct may well have seemed corrupt, if not actually treacherous. So Hsiang Yu took over command himself, and when the news reached the king, far from regarding him as a criminal, he confirmed the appointment.

The Last Stand of the Ch'in

Hsiang Yu immediately put his own plan into action. He sent 20,000 men across the Yellow River to relieve Chu-lu, and when the officers in command reported that they were unable to make headway, he followed them with the rest of the army. When they arrived on the north bank he ensured that they would not think of retreat by sinking all their boats, smashing the cooking pots and burning the temporary huts that had been erected to provide shelter. With no option but to go forward, the Ch'u troops attacked the Ch'in besiegers and fought nine desperate battles before they succeeded in encircling them. The main focus of the fighting seems to have been a road, defended by ramparts on either side, which Chang Han had built from the river to the siege lines in order to transport supplies in safety. No doubt the Ch'in soldiers attempted to use the long walls as field defences, but at the end of the last engagement the road was in Ch'u hands, and all the Ch'in commanders except for Chang Han were either dead or prisoners. Ssu-ma Ch'ien says nothing about any tactical plan that Hsiang Yu might have had, but implies that it was purely a soldier's battle in which victory was determined by the individual fighting qualities of the men on each side. Each Ch'u soldier, we are told, was a match for ten of the enemy, and their battle cries 'reached to Heaven'. The allied contingents camped in the vicinity still took no part in the fighting, but stood on their ramparts and watched. As the battle progressed they became increasingly nervous of the power of the Ch'u army, and we are told that when the Ch'in had been defeated and Hsiang Yu summoned their commanders to his camp, they all obeyed and fell on their knees before him. 'From this moment' says Ssu-ma Ch'ien, 'Hsiang Yu became for the first time supreme general of the feudal states, and the feudal states were all subordinated to him.'

But the war was by no means over, for Chang Han had escaped and remained in the field at the head of a Ch'in army which had so far not been engaged. However Chang was becoming alarmed by political developments in Hsien-yang, where Chao Kao had disposed of his former conspirator Li Ssu and was now in sole control. Chao had sent a message to Chang Han reprimanding him for the defeat at Chu-lu, and had pointedly refused to see an officer who had been sent to the capital for instructions. Afraid that Chao would have him executed, Chang approached Hsiang Yu and negotiated the surrender of his army. Hsiang was now approaching the passes leading to the heartland of Ch'in at the head of a huge allied force drawn from all the newly independent 'feudal states', including an estimated 200,000 Ch'in defectors, who were ordered to form the leading column. However, when they reached the city of Hsin-an, Hsiang received reports that many of the Ch'in recruits were already becoming disaffected. While the dynasty had been in power, Ch'in soldiers had often taken advantage of their position to humiliate and ill-treat the population of the other states, and now the allied troops were taking their revenge, insulting them and treating them as slaves rather than comrades. To forestall a possible mutiny, Hsiang Yu ordered the Ch'in to be massacred. He entrusted this task to his Ch'u soldiers, who had their own scores to settle. They surrounded the Ch'in contingent in their camp at night and murdered them all.

Hsiang Yu resumed his advance, and early in 206 BC reached the Han-ku Pass leading into Ch'in, but found it heavily defended and was forced to regroup. Although diehards continued to resist in the passes, by this time the Ch'in state had virtually disintegrated. Chao Kao had assassinated the Second Emperor Hu-hai and replaced him with a grandson of the First Emperor, Tzu-ying, but the latter had proved to be more strong-willed than expected, and had Chao Kao executed in his turn. King Huai of Ch'u, as supreme commander of the anti-Ch'in alliance, announced that whichever of his generals was the first to break through the passes to Hsien-yang would be granted the city, and the rich farmland of the Wei valley in which it stood, as his personal possession. Hsiang Yu eventually fought his way across the Han-ku Pass at the cost of thousands of casualties, but then came the astounding news that Hsien-yang had already fallen – to an army led by his old comrade-in-arms Liu Pang, the Governor of Pei.

Liu Pang and the Settlement of 206

Liu Pang had so impressed the king in the campaigns of 207 that he had been given an independent command, though still holding an inferior rank to Hsiang Yu. He was notoriously fond of wine and women, but he possessed diplomatic skills and a capacity for calm and rational thought far superior to those of the rash and impatient Hsiang. Liu's great asset as a commander was not his own skill on the battlefield, but his ability to assess the qualities of others, both subordinates and enemies. Tu Mu, a commentator on Sun Tzu, relates an episode from later in his career which illustrates this well. Before launching an attack on Wei, which had reasserted its independence after the collapse of Ch'in, Liu asked his advisors who was in overall command of the Wei armies. 'The reply was "Po Chih". The king (ie. Liu Pang) said; "His mouth still smells of his mother's milk. He cannot equal Han Hsin. Who is the cavalry commander?" The reply was: "Feng Ching". The king said: "He is the son of General Feng Wu-che of Ch'in. Although worthy, he is not the equal of Kuan Ying. And who is the infantry commander?" The reply was: "Hsiang T'o". The king said: "He is no match for Ts'ao Ts'an. I have nothing to worry about."' So Liu despatched the tried and tested trio of Han Hsin, Kuan Ying and Ts'ao Ts'an against Wei, where as predicted they completely outclassed their adversaries and won a rapid victory.

While Hsiang Yu was battering his way through the Han-ku Pass, Liu Pang was leading his smaller army into Ch'in by a less direct route south of the Yellow River, but he was able to make faster progress because he met with little or no resistance. This was not a matter of luck: as Hsiang's spies reported, as soon as he had entered Ch'in territory Liu had forbidden looting, allowed Ch'in officials to remain in their posts, and generally behaved as if he was the legitimate ruler of the country rather than a foreign invader. Belying his own reputation, he had even left the Ch'in women strictly alone. Hsiang Yu, of course, was well aware of what this meant. Liu sent him messages assuring him of his loyalty, and claiming that he had preserved the resources of Ch'in intact only so that he could hand them over to his superior on his arrival, but as one of Hsiang's officers pointed out, it was more likely that he was deliberately courting popularity in Ch'in in order to establish it as his own power base. After all, that was what King Huai had promised to whoever took the objective first. But the king was too far away to intervene, and it was Hsiang Yu who controlled the main Ch'u army on the spot. He is said to have commanded 400,000 men, four times Liu's strength, and his first instinct was to attack his rival and drive him out of Hsien-yang. However his subordinates dissuaded him, pointing out that it was only thanks to Liu's outflanking move that the main army had been able to get through the passes, and that such blatant ingratitude would undermine his own support. For several days the two warlord armies faced each other from their respective fortified positions, while officers with connections in both camps attempted to bring about a diplomatic solution to the crisis. Among these was Yu's uncle, Hsiang Po, whose life had once been saved by Chang Liang, the Marquis of Lu, who was serving in Liu Pang's army. Po went secretly to the enemy camp to warn Chang of his peril, and was persuaded to act as an intermediary between the two commanders. Hsiang Yu professed to accept Liu's declaration of loyalty, and invited him to a meeting.

The next day Liu Pang arrived in his rival's camp at Hung-men with an escort of only a hundred horsemen, and leaving them on guard outside entered the commander's tent with Chang Liang and Hsiang Po. Also present was one of Hsiang Yu's subordinates, Fan Cheng, one of those who had urged the general to take a firm line with Liu. Ssu-ma Ch'ien provides a detailed and dramatic account of what happened in the tent; although he does not name his sources, it presumably came ultimately from Liu Pang himself, or one of his attendants. Fan Cheng was apparently expecting a signal from his chief, and when it did not come he went outside and summoned one of Yu's cousins, Hsiang Chuang, to perform a ceremonial sword dance. The plan was that as soon as he got close enough to Liu Pang, Chuang would use his sword to kill him, but

Hsiang Po unexpectedly joined in the dance, carefully positioning himself so as to protect their guest. Chang Liang realised what was happening, and called in Liu Pang's chariot attendant and personal bodyguard, a formidable warrior named Fan K'uai. K'uai drew his own sword, took up his shield and stormed towards the tent. The sentries on either side of the door crossed their halberds in front of him, but he knocked them both down with his shield and pulled aside the curtain. The dancers stopped, and Hsiang Yu rose to his knees, his hand on his own sword hilt and his eyes wide with fear. Chiang Liang made the introductions and Hsiang Yu offered the newcomer meat and wine, but Fan K'uai, undeterred by his eminent audience, made a speech in which he compared Hsiang Yu's bullying of his subordinates to the tyranny of the First Emperor of Ch'in. Liu Pang, he concluded, deserved to be rewarded for his contribution to victory, not treated with suspicion. Hsiang calmly told Fan to sit down, but Liu Pang realised that the situation was still dangerous, and as soon as opportunity offered he quietly left the tent to relieve himself, explaining that he had drunk too much wine. Then he and his companions ran to their chariot and made their escape. When Hsiang Yu discovered that his plot had been foiled he did not dare to attack the now alerted camp of his rival, but instead allowed his men to sack Hsien-yang in order to deprive Liu Pang of its wealth. In the chaos the last Ch'in ruler, Tzu-ying, was killed, and his palaces burnt to the ground. It was three months before the fires were put out. Liu Pang's reaction is illustrative of his calm, calculating nature; leaving the gold and other treasure to his enemies, he sent an officer into the city to salvage documents, including registers of land ownership, which would be useful in putting a future administration on a firm legal basis. Also retrieved was the First Emperor's map collection, which Liu later put to good use in planning his own strategy.

For the moment, however, Hsiang Yu remained the most powerful warlord in the former Ch'in Empire. He first consolidated his position by arranging the murder of King Huai, then imposed a settlement which seems to have been no more than an attempt to re-establish the old multi-state system of the pre-Ch'in era. He was still reluctant to openly disregard the promises made by Huai, but he contrived to weaken Liu Pang by dividing the former territory of Ch'in into four parts, and placing the richest central area under the control of Chang Han and other renegade Ch'in generals. Liu Pang was allowed to occupy the rough frontier districts of Shu, Pa and Han-chung, to the south of Ch'in proper, which were considered still to be part of the 'Land within The Passes' on the tenuous grounds that many of the people deported by the Ch'in emperors had been sent to live there. From this time onwards Liu's regime came to be known as the Han, after his capital in Han-chung. Hsiang Yu, inevitably, became king of Ch'u, while his leading generals were provided with lands in various parts of the country, apparently without any consideration for local opinion. Not surprisingly the scheme soon backfired. The inhabitants of Ch'in proper, who regarded their new rulers as traitors, expelled them and invited Liu Pang, whose forbearance in the Hsien-yang campaign had obviously been remembered, to take over. Without having to strike a blow, he suddenly found himself in command of the second largest block of territory in China, after Ch'u, and an army which according to Ssu-ma Ch'ien numbered 560,000 men.

The War Resumes

Meanwhile in the spring of 205 BC Hsiang Yu was forced to take his army north-east to Ch'i, where a warlord named T'ien Jung, who had not been allocated any territory under the settlement, had expelled Hsiang Yu's nominees and set himself up as king. Ssu-ma Ch'ien suggests that this whole war was a diversion planned by Liu Pang, who had allowed Hsiang to acquire documents – perhaps forged deliberately for the purpose – implying that T'ien Jung was intending to attack Ch'u. T'ien was defeated and killed, but the Ch'u invaders behaved so badly in Ch'i that they provoked a popular uprising which kept Hsiang Yu busy for the rest of the campaigning season. With the Ch'u forces occupied in the north, Liu Pang struck unexpectedly and captured the city of P'eng-ch'eng, north of the Huai River, which Hsiang was using as his capital and supply base. The Ch'u commander reacted decisively, however, and leaving his main body behind in Ch'i he brought back 30,000 picked troops by forced marches to surprise his enemy. The enormous Han army deployed to meet him, but in a series of engagements the superiority of Hsiang Yu's Ch'u fighters proved decisive. Despite their numerical advantage the Han were driven back in a dawn attack, and Hsiang reoccupied

P'eng-ch'eng. Ssu-ma Ch'ien says that 100,000 Han soldiers were killed when they broke yet again and were driven into two rivers which lay across their rear. They fled south into the mountains, but rallied on the banks of the Sui River near Ling-p'i. Here the chronicler states that another 100,000 Han toops were drowned in the water, blocking the flow of the river with their corpses, but it seems unlikely that they would have allowed the same disaster to happen twice, and Ssu-ma Ch'ien has presumably confused reports of two separate engagements. But whatever happened the Han were unable to hold the repeated Ch'u charges, and Liu Pang's own battlefield skills were clearly not up to the challenge of rallying them again. Soon he found himself abandoned by most of his army, and surrounded by enemies three ranks deep. Luckily for him a storm broke at the crucial moment, driving sand and dust before it which reduced visibility so that 'the day was like night'. Liu broke out in his command chariot under cover of the darkness with only twenty or thirty horsemen, leaving the rest of the army to its fate.

Liu Pang tried to get back to his home town of Pei, but with his friends and relatives in hiding and Hsiang Yu's riders close behind him, he was forced to continue his flight. Liu's father and wife both tried to join him, but ran into the Ch'u army and were captured. At this point in his biography of Hsiang Yu, Ssu-ma Ch'ien tells the story of how, in his panic, Liu twice tried to throw his own son and daughter out of his chariot to lighten the load, only for one of his followers to lift them back in. Eventually he reached Hsia-yi, where his brother-in-law the Marquis of Chou-lu was collecting the fugitives from the defeated army, and where soon afterwards a fresh draft of reinforcements arrived from Ch'in. Liu quickly recovered his nerve and took measures to establish a strong defensive position. By the beginning of 204 BC a strongly fortified camp had been completed at Jung-yang, on the south bank of the Yellow River near a former Ch'in supply depot known as the Ao Granary. A road protected by walls on both sides was also built from the granary to the camp, as the Ch'in had done at Chu-lu, to safeguard food supplies.

The Ch'u pursuit was checked, but when Hsiang Yu arrived at the Ao Granary with his main army he refused an offer of peace and laid siege to the Han position, launching several attacks on the most vulnerable point of the perimeter, the walled road. Liu Pang, however, now felt secure enough to send a detached force under one of his best officers, Han Hsin, to establish a base on the north bank of the Yellow River. Here the old state of Chao had regained its independence under a prince of royal blood who had taken the throne name of King Hsieh. Hsieh had defied Hsiang Yu by replacing the general whom he had placed in command of the territory, but was now attempting to mend relations and ally himself with Ch'u. The only troops available to send with Han Hsin were a motley collection of hastily trained conscripts, but Han was a particularly inspired commander, and several of his battles became famous as examples of the use of cunning to defeat a more numerous enemy. In his first engagement in Chao he employed Sun Pin's technique of pretending that he did not know how to fight. He encountered the army of King Hsieh occupying a fortified position in the Ching-hsing Pass, but he halted his own force several miles short of the mouth of the pass, sending out 2,000 cavalry on a night march to outflank the enemy position. The next morning Han Hsin led 10,000 infantry, comprising the main body of his army, out of camp before breakfast, announcing nonchalantly that the meal would be served once the enemy had been destroyed. He then deployed these troops in leisurely fashion in full view of the enemy, apparently unsupported and with their backs to the River Ti, so that they would be unable to retreat if attacked. King Hsieh had great difficulty in preventing his troops from abandoning their defences and descending on this easy target, but he did not take the bait himself until Han Hsin, with his flags flying and drums beating, went forward and stationed himself well ahead of his front line. Then the Chao soldiers threw caution to the winds and charged, eager to seize the booty which the enemy had foolishly placed within their reach. Han Hsin dropped his flags and drums and fled back to his own lines, while Hsieh's men scattered across the plain, some collecting the loot, others launching a charge against the Han infantry huddled on the riverbank. But these apparently helpless conscripts had been cleverly placed in what Sun Tzu would have called 'death ground' – a situation in which they could not retreat, so had to either fight or die. Out of sheer desperation they fought, and their line held just long enough for their commander's plan to come to fruition. The mounted flanking force had taken up a position on a hill in the Chao rear, from where they could now see that the fortifications in the pass were virtually unoccupied. As ordered, they galloped down and seized them from behind, quickly setting up a row of banners along the ramparts. Before setting out they had been provided with an extra supply of the red flags which distinguished Liu Pang's followers, and now it seemed to the astonished enemy that a huge army had descended behind them and cut off their retreat. Panic spread quickly through the Chao army, and Han Hsin, following up, killed or captured almost all of them. King Hsieh was taken prisoner, and agreed to transfer his allegiance to Liu Pang.

The campaign did not end there, however, because Hsiang Yu's armies in Ch'i had finally succeeded in suppressing the revolt, and marched east to intervene. In his next battle Liu Pang's general Han Hsin employed an even more ingenious stratagem, though Ssu-ma Ch'ien attributes this victory to the cavalry general Kuan Ying, whose idea it may have been. At the Wei River in 203 BC Han Hsin and Kuan Ying were opposed by a combined army from Ch'u and Ch'i led by the Ch'u general Lung Chu, which was drawn up on the west bank of the river to contest the crossing. Aware than his troops were still no match for the men of Ch'u in hand-to-hand combat, Han Hsin sent a detachment of troops upstream under cover of darkness to build a dam with sandbags and block the flow of the river. The rivers of north China are subject to sudden fluctuations in water level, so when the river dropped Lung Chu presumably did not realise that it was anything other than a natural event. At daybreak the Han army crossed the Wei and made a feint attack, then fell back towards the east bank. Lung led the pursuit in person, remarking 'I always knew Han Hsin was a coward!' But when the Han troops reached the shore they rallied and turned to fight, while their comrades upstream broke down the dam. As the water suddenly rose most of the Ch'u soldiers were unable to cross, and their commander, left isolated on the far bank, was surrounded and killed. The Ch'i troops in the allied army promptly deserted, leaving the men of Ch'u with no choice but to retreat. Han Hsin then crossed the river unopposed, and ordered a pursuit in which most of the enemy were overtaken and captured.

By this time, however, Liu Pang had been forced to surrender the Jung-yang position. The enemy had stormed the walled road and cut him off from his food supplies, and his advisor Ch'en P'ing had convinced him that the only practical course was once again to abandon his men and escape to raise another army. This time he was able to buy time by resorting to a typical piece of deception. Fan Tseng, Hsiang Yu's second-in-command, was one of Liu Pang's most implacable enemies, so Liu decided to sow dissension between him and his commander. When a Ch'u messenger arrived in the camp Liu had an ox prepared for a feast, but then the men appointed to serve it pretended to be surprised to find that the emissary had been sent from Hsiang Yu. Announcing that they had supposed that he had come from Fan Tseng, they took the ox away and substituted some inferior food. The messenger, naturally insulted, reported the incident to his commander-in-chief, who assumed not only that Fan was communicating with the enemy, but that he was receiving preferential treatment from them. When Fan was confronted about this he took offence, being of course innocent, and resigned his command. While the Ch'u high command was in disarray, Liu Pang arranged two more diversions. First he sent 2,000 women wearing armour out of the eastern gate of the camp, and the besiegers, mistaking them for an attacking force, concentrated on that side of the defences. Then one of his officers, Chi Hsin, rode out to surrender in a carriage with a yellow canopy, which marked it out as a ruler's personal conveyance. Thinking that he had finally captured Liu Pang, Hsiang Yu was enjoying the congratulations of his troops when it was discovered that the real Han leader had ridden out of the western gate with a small bodyguard and escaped yet again. Chi Hsin paid a heavy price for his part in the scheme, for an infuriated Hsiang had him burnt to death.

Liu Pang crossed the Yellow River, joined up with Han Hsin, and then despatched a small army under P'eng Yueh and Liu Chia to provoke another revolt in Ch'i, which had abandoned its alliance with Ch'u after the defeat at the Wei River. Hsiang Yu took his army east to deal with this new threat, whereupon Liu Pang and Han Hsin returned to the Ao Granary, emptied it of supplies, and then established themselves in another camp at Kuang-wu. The Kuang-wu position was far stronger than that at Jung-yang, as it was surrounded by steep ravines and streambeds which enhanced the fortifications and made an approach difficult in several sectors; the weakness of the supply position had also been remedied by concentrating the grain stores within the camp itself. Hsiang Yu quickly forced P'eng Yueh to retreat and returned to blockade

Liu Pang in his new fortifications, but this time it was Ch'u which faced supply difficulties, as P'eng's army was still in the field and was now placed across the enemy's lines of communication with Ch'u. Hsiang Yu's increasing frustration is illustrated by Ssu-ma Ch'ien's account of the attempts which he now made to bring the war to a close. First he threatened to boil Liu Pang's father alive if he did not surrender, but Liu laughed off the threat, observing that he and Hsiang had sworn to be brothers when they were in the service of King Huai, and so in that sense they shared a father. 'If you insist on boiling your own father' he went on, 'then do me the honour of allotting me a cup of the soup.' Realising that in Liu Pang's case affection towards his own family, and even the traditional Chinese reverence for ancestors, was outweighed by his ambition, Hsiang spared the old man, but proposed instead that the two rivals should settle the fate of the empire by single combat.

Again he was disappointed. Liu Pang declined, saying 'I would rather compete in wisdom, since I cannot compete in strength.' Hsiang Yu then sent forward a champion to challenge the Han to a fight, hoping perhaps to provoke the troops into a rash attack, but Liu responded by despatching one of his own men, an expert archer, who rode out and shot his opposite number dead. He repeated this feat twice more, until Hsiang Yu became so angry that he put on his armour and rode out personally, shouting so fiercely that the archer was intimidated and fled the field. Liu Pang then came forward and the two commanders-in-chief harangued each other from opposite sides of a steep gorge, until Hsiang Yu pulled out a concealed crossbow and shot his adversary, wounding him in the chest. The idea of someone hiding a crossbow about his person may seem bizarre, but small versions of these weapons, ancestors of the modern one-handed 'pistol crossbow', have occasionally been found in tombs of the Warring States period. Hsiang Yu's was probably not a very powerful weapon, for his victim managed to conceal his wound and continued to show himself to his men by walking around the camp, but eventually the pain forced him to retire to his tent.

It is not clear whether Hsiang Yu thought he had killed Liu Pang, but soon afterwards he decided to take a picked force eastwards to deal with P'eng Yueh, leaving three of his subordinates behind to continue the blockade of the Kuang-wu camp. Two of these men, Ts'ao Chiu and Ssu-ma Hsin, were former prison officers who had conspired to release Hsiang Yu when he had been arrested as a young man for some unspecified offence, so they were obviously chosen for their personal loyalty rather than for any military ability. They only had to remain on the defensive for fifteen days, their commander told them, then he would return to organise a final assault. As soon as Hsiang Yu had gone, Liu Pang learned of his departure and began to send messengers to provoke the remaining enemy into attacking. For five or six days they resisted, but at last, disregarding his orders, Ts'ao Chiu led his men out of their field fortifications and across the Ssu River, where the Han defences were weakest. When they were half way across the Han launched their own attack, catching them unprepared and routing them. Ch'u losses were very high, and a great deal of valuable plunder fell into the hands of Liu Pang. Ts'ao Chiu and Ssu-ma Hsin were trapped on the bank of the river, and they both cut their own throats rather than escape to face the wrath of Hsiang Yu.

Hsiang Yu had captured several towns which P'eng Yueh had induced to rebel against him, on this occasion showing uncharacteristic leniency by declining to massacre the inhabitants, but he failed to catch P'eng himself and returned frustrated to Kuang-wu. The victorious Han had emerged from their camp and laid siege to a nearby town, but on Hsiang's approach they again withdrew. Liu Pang was still not prepared to face his rival in a pitched battle, but the Ch'u supply situation was worse than ever. So many men had been lost at the Ssu River that further offensive operations were impossible. Hsiang therefore reluctantly agreed to make peace. Liu's captive relatives were set free, and the two men divided the empire between them, with the Hung Canal as the boundary. All the land west of that line was allocated to Han, while everything to the east was to belong to Ch'u.

The Final Campaign

According to Ssu-ma Ch'ien, it was two of Liu Pang's advisors, Chiang Liang and Ch'en P'ing, who persuaded him to break the peace agreement and seize the opportunity to finish off his rival once and for all. Han, they argued, was now in a position of strength, in possession of the richest part of the Empire, and with most of the feudal lords of the north now owing it allegiance thanks to Han Hsin's campaigns. Ch'u, on the other hand, was suffering from famine and war-weariness, and Hsiang Yu had begun to alienate many of his followers by his insistence on keeping all the honours and riches gained in his wars for himself. Nevertheless this favourable state of affairs was unlikely to last. Chiang and Ch'en compared Liu Pang's situation to that of a man who buys himself a brief respite by feeding a starving tiger, but leaves himself with perils for the future once the tiger has recovered its strength. So early in 202 BC, 'the fifth year of the Han dynasty' by Ssu-ma Ch'ien's reckoning, Liu Pang set his armies in motion once again. The plan was for him to advance beyond the town of Yang-hsia to Ku-ling, then to take up a defensive position and wait for the armies of Han Hsin and P'eng Yueh to join him. Presumably the intention was that the Han forces should march as separate corps while in friendly territory to ease the supply situation, then rendezvous for a decisive battle once they had advanced so far that Hsiang Yu would have no choice but to fight.

It is an indication of the sophistication of Chinese military strategy in this period that such a manoeuvre could be contemplated. Few European armies before the age of Napoleon could have carried it off successfully. But the obstacle to success in Liu Pang's case was not military but political. Liu arrived at Ku-ling to find no sign of his allied armies. Instead he met Hsiang Yu with the full muster of Ch'u, and in the ensuing battle the Han were, as usual, badly defeated. Liu fell back into his camp and hurriedly fortified it with ditches and ramparts, but just as in previous years Hsiang Yu, though still capable of winning a pitched battle, lacked the strength to take the camp by assault. Instead he built a fortified camp of his own at nearby Kai-hsia, and settled down to blockade the invaders. Meanwhile in the Han camp, speculation must have been rife. Had Liu Pang been betrayed, or had his lieutenants merely been accidentally delayed? Days passed with no sign of the relieving forces. At last Liu consulted Chiang Liang, who pointed out that Han Hsin and P'eng Yueh had been provided with no incentive to act decisively. Although the aim of the campaign was to eliminate Ch'u and take over its enormous territory, the two men had not been offered any reward for their assistance. Chiang suggested that messengers should be sent promising them large grants of land, 'to make sure that each is fighting for himself'. So Liu Pang decreed that 'When Ch'u has been defeated, the land to the east of Ch'en as far as the sea shall be given to the King of Ch'i (i.e. Han Hsin), and the land to the north of Sui-yang as far as Ku-ch'eng shall be given to Chief minister P'eng.' Sure enough the messengers returned with the news that the armies were on the march. What was more, on the way they gathered support from other local magnates, no doubt eager to ensure their own share of the spoils. Han Hsin was joined by an army under Liu Jia, which proved its loyalty by slaughtering the pro-Ch'u population of Ch'eng-fu. Chou Yin, the Grand Marshal of Ch'u, also defected to the invaders, and followed Liu Jia and P'eng Yueh at the head of his own contingent.

Encirclement at Kai-Hsia

Hsiang Yu now found himself besieged in his turn by five armies drawn from all corners of the Empire. Ssu-ma Ch'ien tells us that the Han and their allies were numerous enough to encircle the entire enemy camp with a battle line several men deep. But what finally demoralised the Ch'u commander was the apparent presence in the enemy camp of men from his own country. Each night, we are told, the invaders entertained themselves with singing, among which could be heard the traditional songs of Ch'u. Different sources give varying explanations for this. Many of Liu Pang's men had previously campaigned in Ch'u and may have adopted popular songs from the enemy, as soldiers have done throughout the ages. No doubt Chou Yin's men also introduced their own favourites. But Hsiang Yu immediately came to the conclusion that his own men were deserting. This episode shows more starkly than any other the weakness of Hsiang's character. He was clearly a battlefield commander of genuine talent, superior to Liu Pang, but he was unstable and he lacked his opponent's determination in adversity. His response to any setback was either to fly into a rage or, as here, to lose his head completely. On hearing the singing, he exclaimed 'Has Han already taken the whole of Ch'u?' Then he retired into his tent with a concubine named Yu and got drunk, composing and singing his own epitaph, and that of his favourite horse Chui, or 'Dapple'. Ssu-ma Ch'ien quotes one verse as follows:

My strength plucked up mountains
And my energies overshadowed the world,
But the times were not favourable,
And Chui will not sally forth again.
If Chui does not sally forth again
Alas, what can be done?
Ah Yu! Ah Yu!
What will become of you?

No doubt if he had applied his talents to the defence of the camp the Han forces would have suffered heavy losses in trying to take it, and may even have been forced back to the negotiating table. It is obvious that there were still simmering tensions among the allies – several of whom were very recent recruits to the cause – which could have been exploited. But now Hsiang Yu thought only of escape. He gathered together under his banner a picked bodyguard of more than 800 cavalrymen, and as soon as darkness fell he broke through the besieging lines and rode away south-eastwards in the direction of the Ch'u homeland, abandoning the rest of the army to its fate just as his rival had so often done. The difference this time was that Hsiang had no more troops to replace them. The relative ineptitude of the Han soldiers is shown by the fact that, according to Ssu-ma Ch'ien, Liu Pang was not made aware of the breakout until the next morning. What happened to the Han officer in charge of the sector involved we are not told, but Liu immediately ordered Cavalry General Kuan Ying to take 5,000 horsemen in pursuit. Meanwhile Hsiang Yu had crossed the River Huai, although the pace had been too much for most of his followers, and allegedly only a hundred men now remained with him. The figures used in the remainder of this account are Ssu-ma Ch'ien's, but it is obvious that they are even less reliable than usual. They greatly exaggerate the number of casualties inflicted by the Ch'u cavalry, and it is likely that they also understate Hsiang Yu's remaining strength, as it is hardly plausible that such a small band of fugitives could have held out for so long against overwhelming numbers. No doubt the historian relied for this part of his narrative on a pro-Ch'u source which was keen to emphasise the heroic last fight of the great commander. But it is still necessary to bear in mind that the Han soldiers had never been able to defeat their Ch'u counterparts when led by Hsiang Yu in open battle without either having a great advantage in numbers, or using what might be considered trickery. What Hsiang might still have achieved at the head of his entire army we can only speculate.

The fugitives remained comfortably ahead of their pursuers as far as a place called Yin-ling, but there their leader became lost and asked a local peasant for directions. The latter, obviously a Han loyalist, directed him away from the road to the left, or east, where his horses became mired in a marsh and valuable time was lost. Once they had extricated themselves the Ch'u cavalry continued eastwards, but according to Ssu-ma Ch'ien only twenty-eight troopers were still with him. Whether the others had deserted or been overtaken by the Han is not clear, but Kuan Ying's force must by now have been catching up fast, because at Tung-ch'eng Hsiang Yu stopped to make a stand. Here Ssu-ma Ch'ien reports him making a self-justifying speech, in which he claimed never to have been defeated in eight years of warfare and more than seventy battles. Therefore, he argued, the decline in his fortunes could not have been due to any fault of his own, but had come about because Heaven had inexplicably withdrawn its favour. He accepted that he would die that day, but he would prove his point by inflicting one last defeat on his enemies, despite the enormous disparity in numbers. He would break through the encircling Han horsemen, cut down their flag and behead one of their generals: 'so that you, my lords, will understand that it is Heaven that is destroying me, and that it is not that I have done anything wrong in battle.'

He drew up his tiny force on top of a hill in four sections, facing in all directions, as the Han cavalrymen arrived and surrounded his position. Then, after establishing three rallying points back on the hill, he led a wild downhill charge which scattered the enemy, who had perhaps not had time to deploy properly after their headlong pursuit. As Hsiang Yu had predicted, one of the Han generals was caught and decapitated in the rout. Kuan Ying himself rode up to confront the Ch'u commander, but the latter is said to have glared and shouted so fiercely that Kuan Ying's horse took fright and bolted, carrying him ignominiously out of the fight. Then the Ch'u warriors returned to the hill and formed into three separate groups, each of which was soon once again surrounded by the Han cavalry. Hsiang attacked a second time, killing another enemy officer and, in Ssu-ma Ch'ien's account, nearly a hundred of his men in exchange for only two Ch'u casualties. Then, instead of returning to the hill, he led his surviving troopers off again on a headlong gallop for the banks of the River Wu. If the historian's casualty figures are anywhere correct – which seems unlikely – the Han must have been too cowed by the reputation of their opponents to put up much resistance. But they rallied yet again, and the dogged pursuit continued.

At the river the fugitives encountered a local headman who was waiting for them with a boat. This suggests that a rendezvous may have been arranged in advance, but there was only one boat, and apparently no room for anyone but Hsiang Yu himself. The headman begged him to cross the river, pointing out that at least for a time he would be safe from his enemies, and that the people, numbering several hundred thousand, were still loyal to Ch'u and would willingly make him their king. But Hsiang had had enough of running. He explained that he had led 8,000 young men west over the Wu for the war against Han, and that if he now returned without a single one of them he would hardly be able to look their families in the face. His pursuers were once again in sight and closing in. So he gave his horse Chui to his would-be rescuer, ordered his men to dismount and draw their swords, and led a suicidal charge on foot. Having suffered ten wounds, and again killed 'several hundred' men single-handed, the Ch'u general spotted an old comrade in arms, Lu Ma-t'ong, in the enemy ranks. Shouting out to Lu that he knew that there was a large reward on his head and so he would do his old friend a favour, Hsiang Yu then cut his own throat. Ssu-ma Ch'ien tells how the Han soldiers trampled each other in a rush to get at the body and acquire pieces of it as proof of their prowess. Wang Yi collected the head, and four other officers – including Lu Ma-t'ong – each cut off a limb to take back to Liu Pang. All five were eventually rewarded with high rank and extensive estates. After the death of Hsiang Yu the whole of China quickly submitted to Liu Pang, with the exception of the old city state of Lu, of which the Ch'u leader had once been given the honorary title of Duke by the Ch'u king. The Han armies were already deployed for one last campaign when someone had the idea of displaying Hsiang's severed head, to convince the diehard defenders that he really was dead. This seems to have persuaded the chiefs of Lu to surrender, so escaping the otherwise inevitable slaughter. In an echo of the old chivalrous attitudes which had almost disappeared under the Ch'in onslaught, Liu Pang therefore gave permission for his old rival's remains to be given an honourable burial, with the ceremonies that had been due to a Duke of Lu under the ancient rules of the Chou.

Chapter Five

China Versus Rome? The Han Campaigns in the Far West, 200 BC to AD 100

'The implements for attack and defence each have their own categories. This results in the great awesomeness of the army.' The *Six Secret Teachings* of the T'ai Kung.

Immediately after his victory in 202 BC Liu Pang adopted the title of Emperor Kao-ti of the Han dynasty. His court was established at Ch'ang-an in the Wei valley, near the site of the former Ch'in capital of Hsien-yang. Kao-ti based much of his government on the precedent set by the militaristic Ch'in, but he also brought a much-needed stability, which gained the loyalty of his people and ensured the survival of his line for more than four centuries. What later became known as the Early or 'Western' Han remained in power until AD 8, when a rebel named Wang Mang established the short-lived Hsin dynasty, only to be overthrown by Han loyalists seventeen years later. The Later or 'Eastern' Han then ruled from AD 25 until its final collapse under the pressures of internal revolts and barbarian invasions after 189. In its day Han China was one of the two great powers of the Eurasian continent, rivalled only by Imperial Rome, and it was under the rule of the Han that China began to break out of its geographical isolation for the first time since those unknown charioteers had brought their invention east to the court of the Shang kings, and reach out towards the wider world.

The process was by no means a peaceful one. Indeed, since before the rise of the Ch'in the greatest military problem facing the Chinese states had been the security of their northern frontiers, beyond which the nomadic steppe tribes had now perfected the combination of equestrianism and bowmanship to produce the most formidable weapons system known to the ancient world – the mounted archer. By the time the Ch'in came to power the most powerful of these tribes, the Hsiung-nu, had established an empire which was the rival of China in territory and military strength, if not in population. The deserts and steppes of what is now Mongolia never could support a population as large as that of agricultural China, but the Hsiung-nu horse-archers made up for this by the mobility and fighting skills for which the Central Asian nomads have always been famous. These are well illustrated by an encounter described by Ssu-ma Ch'ien, which took place on the steppe between three Hsiung-nu eagle hunters and ten times their number of Chinese cavalry. The latter, apparently lacking bows, were unable to come to close quarters with their fast moving opponents, who wheeled away every time they were charged, circled round and picked most of them off with arrows, eventually forcing the survivors to flee. The Han naturally recruited as many of these nomads as they could get, but the bulk of their armies, like those of the Ch'in, consisted of infantry, with smaller numbers of cavalry and heavy chariots. These suffered from a number of disadvantages in the frontier wars against the Hsiung-nu, one of which was that they were too numerous to live off the land, and so had to operate at the end of long and vulnerable supply lines. It was calculated that no Chinese army could campaign on the northern steppes for more than a hundred days, because of the difficulties of bringing up rations, horse fodder and firewood in wagons drawn by oxen, who themselves needed to be fed on what they brought with them. By contrast the Hsiung-nu ponies could survive indefinitely on grass, and their riders on the milk and meat provided by their mobile herds. The Han might win in a pitched battle while their troops were fresh and well supplied, but the enemy could skirmish with their bows from a distance, avoiding battle until exhaustion and attrition had worn them down, then attack at a time and place of their own choosing.

The Han Army

Nevertheless, whether fighting on its own ground or in the wastes of Central Asia, the Han army was undoubtedly a formidable force. Some units were formed from volunteers, and a military career with them – especially in the cavalry – was still a respectable choice for the sons of the nobility. Several elite Imperial Guard cavalry units are known, distinguished by titles like 'Brave as Tigers'. Under later dynasties the pacifist influence of Confucianism eventually undermined the prestige of the army, but in Han times this was still far in the future. However the bulk of the armies consisted of conscripts or amnestied prisoners, who were available in very large numbers, but whose levels of training and enthusiasm could vary dramatically. A defeat by the Hsiung-nu in 129 BC, for example, was blamed on conscript troops who had been hastily committed to battle without proper training. On the other hand, under inspired leadership the same men could fight heroically. Li Kuang-li's forces in the 'Heavenly Horses' expeditions to Ferghana, described below, were formed mostly of freed convicts and young men of 'bad reputation', but performed staggering feats of marching and fighting under very difficult conditions.

Surviving documents from the forts established on the north-western frontier tell us that garrison troops at least were organised into 'sui' or squads, each with an officer and between four and ten men. A variable number of squads would form a 'hou' or platoon, of which five made up a company, 'hou kuan' (Loewe). The regular appearance of multiples of five in Han infantry organisations implies that the standard battle formation may still have been five men deep, as it had been since the Shang dynasty. The conscripts fought as infantry, armed with swords, spears or dagger-axes, or with bows or crossbows. Most Han footsoldiers depicted in art appear to be unarmoured, but others show that lamellar armour remained in use. The typical Han body armour was a slightly simplified version of the Ch'in style, known as 'liang-tang' or 'double-faced', because it consisted of identical pieces for the front and back of the torso, connected by shoulder straps. Some tomb figures, however, continue to depict a more comprehensive lamellar coat covering the shoulders and upper arms, with a scarf worn around the neck to prevent the armour chafing, and perhaps to provide additional light protection for the throat. Excavated helmets are often also made of metal strips rivetted together, which would have been lighter and more flexible than the old solid bronze versions. Crossbows seem now to have been the most common missile weapons, and were often employed by specialists known as 'chueh chang', chosen for the physical strength needed to bend the powerful bows. The crossbow remained unknown to the Central Asian tribes; it was said by the Chinese that even if examples were captured, the trigger mechanism was so precisely engineered that the 'barbarians' would be unable to copy it. In fact many of the peoples of the steppe were skilled metal workers, and could surely have produced such a device if they had wished. Probably their mounted archers were perfectly happy with their composite bows, which were easier to handle on horseback, and made up in rate of shooting what they might theoretically have lacked in penetrating power. Some Chinese also fought as lightly equipped mounted archers, copying the nomads who had been their original inspiration, but most horse-archers were now recruited from friendly steppe tribes. Other Chinese cavalry wore similar armour to the infantry and fought mainly with swords, though dagger-axes, spears, bows, and even crossbows could also be wielded from horseback.

First Forays into Central Asia

As early as 200 BC the Emperor Kao-ti had encountered the problem of dealing with horse-archer armies when he led an army in pursuit of some Hsiung-nu raiders, only to find himself ambushed and his lines of communication cut by hordes of light cavalry. He extricated his army by buying the enemy off with tribute and the promise of a Han princess in marriage for their ruler, and after this an uneasy peace endured for several decades. In 138 BC, however, the Emperor Wu-ti reversed the policy of appeasement. He had received reports of another tribe known as the Yueh-chih, who lived far to the west, and were said to be mortal enemies of the Hsiung-nu. A young officer named Chang Ch'ien was sent to contact them and returned thirteen years later after many adventures, having escaped twice from Hsiung-nu captivity. The Yueh-chih had turned out to be reluctant to join in a war, but Chang had established relations with several other Central Asian peoples who were keen to open relations with China. Best of all, they seemed to offer a tactical solution to the Hsiung-nu problem. As Ssu-ma-Ch'ien reported, the people of Ferghana, for example, lived in walled cities, grew crops and numbered in the hundreds of thousands, but they retained the fighting traditions of their nomadic ancestors and 'can shoot arrows while on horseback'. The horses of Ferghana were so superior to the Han mounts that they were known as 'Heavenly Horses'. Acquiring a supply became a major aim of Chinese policy in Central Asia, but despite their apparent friendliness the rulers of Ferghana refused to part with what they must have realised was a vital strategic asset. Nevertheless Wu-ti ordered a massive surprise attack on the unsuspecting Hsiung-nu, which drove them out of the region known as the Ordos, or 'Place of Tents', in the great loop of the Yellow River where the cultivated land met the steppe. This gain was consolidated by settling hundreds of thousands of Chinese farmers in the Ordos, and from this advanced base a series of expeditions was sent west to open the road to Ferghana. Between 121 and 119 BC cavalry armies under Wei Ch'ing and Huo Ch'u-p'ing defeated five Hsiung-nu chiefdoms along the border and forced them to submit, and in 108 BC the important trading centre of Turfan, on the Silk Route to the west, was occupied by a Chinese garrison. Already the silk trade with Rome and the Middle East was becoming an important source of revenue for China, even though it was carried out by Central Asian middlemen, and the producers and customers at either end of the route had no direct contact with each other. Now the lure of trade, as well as military strategy, was drawing the Chinese westwards.

The Heavenly Horses

Four years after the capture of the city, with the Hsiung-nu still in disarray, an army of 20,000 Chinese and 6,000 nomad allies, led by Li Kuang-li, crossed the Takla Makan desert from Turfan to Ferghana with the aim of bringing back a herd of the 'Heavenly Horses'. This first attempt failed, because the city states along the route refused to provide supplies and Li's starving army was easily driven off by the Ferghanans. Another problem that may not have been foreseen was the effect of altitude sickness when crossing the high passes across the Pamir Mountains. These passes were more than 12,000 feet above sea level, well above the point at which unacclimatised men from the lowlands were likely to be affected. In fact the first account of this condition appears in a Chinese text of about 35 BC, describing what may be the same route: 'On passing the Great Headache Mountain, the Little Headache Mountain, the Red Land and the Fever Slope, men's bodies become feverish, they lose colour and are attacked with headache and vomiting'. Baggage animals, we are told, suffered similarly. It would not be surprising if an army marching by this route was unfit for combat until it had had the chance to recuperate at lower altitude. Li nevertheless risked execution for his failure when he returned to the court in Ch'ang-an, but he managed to talk his way out of trouble. The problem, he argued, was that he had not been given enough men. If a small army had starved there did not seem to be much hope for a bigger one, but the emperor agreed to send him back, this time at the head of a much larger expedition comprising 60,000 troops. Li turned out to be right, because the local citizens were so intimidated by this huge force that they opened their gates without argument and provided all the supplies needed. Half of the men still died or deserted, but those who remained were sufficient to defeat the king of Ferghana and bring back 3,000 captured horses. These formed the basis of stud farms which improved the old Chinese breed, and in the long run greatly increased the power of the Chinese cavalry.

This was not the end of the wars with the Hsiung-nu, however, and after 99 BC the balance again swung in favour of the nomads. That year saw the defeat of a Han army under Li Ling, an ambitious tactical theorist who had devised methods which he believed would enable infantry to defeat the horse-archers without the help of cavalry. He had been ordered to take 5,000 Chinese footsoldiers and their supply wagons to a rendezvous with a force of cavalry under Liu Po-te before advancing into the steppe, but the two officers were on bad terms and Liu, who had protested against being placed under Li's orders, failed to turn up. Li therefore marched without cavalry support, but as he approached the T'ien Shan Mountains he was intercepted by an army of 30,000 Hsiung-nu mounted archers. He drew up his men in the saddle between two hills behind a barrier of wagons, with men armed with spears and shields in front, and crossbowmen shooting overhead from the rear ranks. The Hsiung-nu launched several attacks, but were beaten off each time by the crossbows, leaving thousands dead on the field. However Li quickly ran short of ammunition, and with the enemy still in force across his supply lines he had no choice but to retreat. At first his little army did so in good order, but the Hsiung-nu easily outdistanced him, and as he marched through a narrow ravine not far from the frontier he ran into an ambush. Some of the enemy blocked the road ahead, while others rolled down rocks from the slopes on either side. Many of Li's men fled, but 3,000 of them rallied round their commander and fought on. The crossbowmen abandoned their weapons after shooting off their remaining bolts, and used the axles from the wagons as improvised spears. When night fell Li ordered the survivors to split up into small parties and make for the frontier posts, but only 400 of them ever reached safety. Li Ling was not among them; he had been spotted and taken prisoner by the Hsiung-nu. From a purely tactical point of view his ideas had perhaps been vindicated, but he had only succeeded in proving that, although they could mount a successful defence against mounted archers, unsupported infantry could not secure their own supply lines or prevent themselves being surrounded on the open grassland. Neither could they bring a more mobile enemy to battle except on the enemy's own terms. After this debacle the great western campaigns were abandoned, and it was not until many years later, after the Hsiung-nu empire split into northern and southern factions in AD 49, that the Han managed to regain their Central Asian possessions.

The Battle of Kang-chu, 36 BC

Relations between the Han and the Hsiung-nu nevertheless remained strained during the intervening period, and numerous small scale actions took place involving provincial Chinese forces stationed on the northern and western frontiers. One of these, the Kang-chu campaign of 36 BC, is described in exceptional detail in the Han sources, and although it was of only local significance, it is worth recounting as an example of the tactics used by the Chinese and their enemies. The Hsiung-nu Empire had recently been thrown into turmoil as rival claimants contended for the title of Shan-yu, or Emperor, and one of these contending warlords, a man whom we know only by his Chinese name of Chih Chih, had sought refuge in the region of Kang-chu in Sogdiana. There he recruited an army which seems to have consisted mainly of local Central Asians, and set out to establish his new state on a firm economic basis by stealing livestock from the neighbouring nomad tribes. His victims included the

Wu-sun, who were officially allies of the Han, and who sent a message to Kan Yen-shou, the Protector General of the Western Regions, begging for help.

At the time Kan was ill, so the message was received by his second-in-command, Ch'en T'ang. Ch'en apparently believed that Chih Chih posed an urgent threat to the trade routes with the west, and so decided not to wait for instructions from the imperial authorities. Instead he forged an imperial decree authorising him to raise troops, and prepared to lead them west. Before he could depart Kan Yen-shou returned to duty, but instead of punishing his subordinate for his illegal action, he supported him and agreed to lead the expedition in person. In view of the harsh penalties normally imposed by the Han emperors for insubordination or failure, both men were obviously taking a serious risk, but they may have considered that in the prevailing political climate imperial approval for a war was unlikely to be forthcoming. However, if they were seen not to be able to respond to a provocation like Chih Chih's, their own prestige among China's allies in Central Asia might be undermined. Altogether they are said to have raised 40,000 men, whom they led west in two separate columns, one north and one south of the Takla Makan Desert. No doubt this plan was adopted to minimise supply difficulties, but by the time they rendezvoused on the far side of the Pamir passes food was nevertheless running short, and the men had suffered severely from the cold; Kan himself returned home permanently disfigured as a result of frostbite. Possibly Chih Chih had counted on these factors to prevent any further advance, but if so he had made a serious miscalculation. The herds of cattle, sheep and horses which he had stolen from the Wu-sun were grazing on the meadows west of the mountains when the Han columns arrived unexpectedly, overwhelmed the surprised guards and rounded up the animals, instantly resolving their supply difficulties. The account of the subsequent battle mentions only Chinese infantry, but this episode suggests that they must have been accompanied by a substantial force of cavalry, as surely only mounted troops would have been able to overtake the nomad herdsmen.

Chih Chih withdrew into a fortified town on the Tu-lai River and awaited the attack. The position was defended by an earth wall, outside which was a wooden palisade manned by archers and covered by a ditch. Beyond this, according to the Chinese, were stationed a hundred local Sogdian cavalry and a hundred infantry, the latter drawn up in what is described as 'fish-scale' formation. This term might refer to the way their shields overlapped when they drew up in close order. On the other hand Chang Yu, a Sung period commentator on Sun Tzu, uses the term 'fish scale' for a formation consisting of chariots in the front rank and infantry behind them, so possibly all that is meant here is that the infantry were behind the cavalry. In any case it seems that for once the numbers of the enemy were understated, because such a small force could hardly have been expected to prevail against the Chinese army, even if Kan and Ch'en's men numbered considerably less than the claimed 40,000. In any case the cavalry launched a charge on the invaders as they halted to set up camp, but were repulsed by the Han crossbowmen. The fate of Chih Chih's infantry is uncertain. The eminent scholar Homer Dubs once proposed a theory, since widely repeated, that they were in fact Roman legionaries. According to this scenario, soldiers of the army of Crassus, captured by the Parthians at the Battle of Carrhae in 53 BC, might have been transported east to Sogdiana, where they were somehow subverted or taken prisoner by Chih Chih. These remarkably unsuccessful legionaries are supposed to have been captured yet again in this engagement and taken back by Kan and Ch'en to the western frontier of China, where they were used to garrison a city called Li Kan – a name which was also used in Han writings for the mysterious lands of the far west. If this theory was correct these anonymous Romans would have been the first people in history known to have travelled almost the entire length of the Eurasian continent from east to west, but unfortunately it is based on a very tenuous line of argument. Dubs identified the men at Kang-chu as Romans simply because they fought as infantry, in the 'fish scale' formation which he considered to be the equivalent of a Roman 'testudo', and their base was defended with a ditch and wooden palisade in a fashion which also reminded him of Roman practice. But there is no reason why the city states of Central Asia should not also have fielded infantry, and the use of field fortifications was hardly a Roman monopoly. As for the overlapping shields, even if that is in fact what the fish scale simile meant, they could simply have been an ad hoc response to the threat of the enemy crossbows.

Whoever the infantry opposing them really were, the Chinese troops appear to have experienced little difficulty in disposing of them, and they are not mentioned again in the Han account. The attackers are next described advancing against the palisade surrounding the town, with men carrying 'great shields' in the front rank, and spearmen and crossbowmen behind. The latter provided covering fire with a series of volleys which eventually drove the Sogdian archers from their positions. Assault detachments then ran forward, drained the ditch, and stacked firewood against the outside of the palisade. Then they set fire to it, while Chih Chih attempted to rally his troops behind the earth walls of the town itself. That night a relief column of 10,000 Sogdian cavalry arrived and attacked the Han camp, but after several unsuccessful charges they appear to have abandoned the attempt. Meanwhile the assault on the town continued despite the darkness. Resistance centred on a tall tower in Chih Chih's palace where he had taken refuge with the women of his harem, and from which he attempted to shoot arrows at the besiegers. Neither side can have been able to shoot accurately in the darkness, but the massed volleys of the Chinese crossbows eventually proved decisive. Many of the women hiding in the tower were killed, and at last Chih Chih was felled by a bolt which struck him on the nose. As dawn broke the Han infantry fought their way into the town and set fire to the palace. In the confusion the tower was stormed, and the wounded Chih Chih was stabbed to death. His head was then taken as proof of the victory. When news of the campaign reached Ch'ang-an, the emperor debated whether Kan and Ch'en should be executed for the offence of forging official documents and raising an illegal army, but in view of their success, and its effect on the reputation of the Han in Central Asia, they were pardoned. The usual rewards given to successful generals were withheld, however, for fear of encouraging other officers to launch similar risky expeditions without orders.

Pan Chao

The main architect of the new wave of imperialism under the later Han was another swashbuckling adventurer, Pan Chao, who led his first expedition west in AD 73. Recruiting Central Asian allies was always a difficult diplomatic balancing act, because they had to be persuaded that the small Chinese forces in the west represented a power strong enough to be worth co-operating with, but not one so overbearing as to be a threat to their independence. Pan Chao was an expert at this, but he was also capable of great ruthlessness where necessary. The ruler of the first city state he came to, Shan-shan, planned to betray him to the southern Hsiung-nu, but the Chinese commander was informed of the plot and set fire to the city, massacring both the locals and the Hsiung-nu emissaries under cover of the flames. For the next thirty years Pan Chao campaigned along the Silk Route, often operating as an effectively independent power. Eventually he brought fifty tribes under Han authority, and earned from an appreciative emperor the title of 'Protector General of the Western Regions'. His most significant achievement began when he made an alliance with the Yueh-chih, who since Chang Ch'ien's day had developed into a powerful nation known as the Kushans, said to be capable of mobilising an army of 70,000 men. Via the Kushans contact was made with the Parthian Empire further west, and from the Parthians Pan Chao learned of an even greater power which he called Ta-ch'in, situated on the shore of a great western sea. This was Syria, at the eastern end of the Mediterranean and then part of the Roman Empire. In AD 97 Pan despatched an officer named Kan Ying to find out more about this mysterious empire, but the Parthians seem to have deliberately led him astray, no doubt to prevent the loss of their lucrative position as middlemen in the silk trade. They took him to a sea port, possibly on the Persian Gulf, and told him that from there the voyage to Ta-ch'in would take two years. So a discouraged Kan Ying abandoned the mission. On his return he provided Pan Chao with a fairly accurate report on the Roman Empire, but no further attempts were ever made to travel there.

Kan Ying's expedition especially has always been of interest to western historians, who are understandably fascinated by the possibility of a clash between the two great empires of Eurasia. The legions of Rome and the famous crossbowmen of Han dominated their respective theatres, both using – in different ways – the industrial and manpower resources of a great settled civilisation to overcome their warlike 'barbarian' neighbours. And yet – if we discount the Kang-chu affair – they were never tested against each other. Would the crossbows have defeated the Roman shields and armour, or would the legionary swordsmen have swept all before them, as they were accustomed to doing in the west? On neutral ground it might have been a very close run thing. But in reality neither army could get at the other across the intervening deserts of Central Asia without undergoing some major modifications. The expeditions that Pan Chao led into the west were made up largely of allies from Ferghana and the cities of the Tarim Basin. Even these seldom moved far beyond the eastern borders of Parthia, and it seems that Kan Ying's mission to the Mediterranean coast was a diplomatic rather than a strictly military one, probably escorted by Parthian soldiers rather than Chinese. Even when Trajan's legions carried the Roman eagles further east than they had ever been before in their invasion of Parthia in AD 116, regular Roman and Chinese military units may never have come within a thousand miles of each other. So one of the great 'might have beens' of history never came to pass.

At the same time as Pan Chao was pushing towards the west, other Han commanders were taking the offensive against the northern Hsiung-nu horde, this time with the aid of allies recruited from among their southern rivals, as well as the Wu-huan and Hsien-pi, also nomadic tribes who had previously been Hsiung-nu vassals. In AD 89 a combined Han and nomad army defeated the northerners at Mount Ch'i-lo on the Mongolian steppe. Unfortunately, though, in the long run this victory only succeeded in replacing the Hsiung-nu with the equally dangerous Hsien-pi, who demanded ever greater 'rewards' for their co-operation, and launched destructive raids into China when they did not receive them. Then the Ch'iang of the south-west, foot-fighting tribes related to the Tibetans, also began to move into China, and by AD 140 they had linked up with the nomads to the north and forced the Han garrisons to abandon the towns along the Silk Route. The tide had turned yet again, and the Chinese presence in Central Asia was not to be restored for half a millennium.

Chapter Six

The Struggle for the T'ong Pass, AD 537 to 547

'The northern barbarians are fierce and stupid, like wild birds or beasts. Their strength is fighting in the open fields; their weakness is in attacking walls.' Kao Lu of the Northern Wei.

The Fall of the Han and the Barbarian Invasions

In its various incarnations the Han dynasty controlled China for nearly four hundred years, overseeing one of its greatest eras of territorial expansion as well as economic and cultural progress. In the rest of the world it is by far the best known period of pre-modern Chinese history, while within the country the people are still proud to describe themselves as 'sons of Han'. But eventually this great imperial dynasty suffered the fate common to all those who tried to rule such an enormous area in the days before modern transport and communications. Officially the Eastern Han remained in power until AD 220, but long before then the titles of its emperors were little more than a façade. Here began the successive cycles of unification and disintegration which have characterised the last two millennia of Chinese history. First a strong leader would overthrow his predecessors by force and establish a centralised government, then there would ensue a period of imperial expansion, followed by a gradual decline in the quality of the rulers and the degree of control which they were able to exert over the regions. Finally the empire would collapse into chaos as rival warlords struggled for power, leading to a period of political fragmentation until a new conqueror arose, and the whole cycle began again.

The Chinese, taking their cue from the explanation provided long before by the Chou for their defeat of the Shang, have traditionally seen this process in terms of a 'Mandate of Heaven', which was given to a dynasty as long as its rulers possessed the virtues needed to govern the empire, and was withdrawn when they declined too far from the standards set by the founder. Heaven might show its disapproval by popular unrest and natural disasters, and a series of the latter could undermine public confidence in the regime. But even at the best of times the conflicting forces of centralisation and regionalism made China a difficult country to rule. It covered a vast area, divided by numerous mountain ranges and great rivers, and the frontiers of the Han Empire in the south were many weeks away by horse or boat from the political centre in the north-west. Often these frontiers could only be defended by allowing considerable autonomy to the commanders on the spot, who developed into semi-independent warlords whose armies were loyal to them personally rather than to the distant emperor. China was also culturally diverse, and the people of the north and those of the south often despised and distrusted one another just as they had done in the days of Duke Wen. Since Chou times the concept of a single unified empire had been widely accepted in theory, but this did not necessarily imply that the emperor enjoyed absolute power, free from the obligations to rule in accordance with tradition and consider the welfare of their subjects. The fate of the Ch'in, whose rulers did believe in unfettered absolutism, was remembered as a warning to future dynasties. So as soon as a regime began to lose its grip, it was almost inevitable that one of its generals would challenge its legitimacy, claiming Heaven's mandate for themselves and attempting to found a successor dynasty.

After AD 189 the Han empire split apart, and its territories were divided among the 'Three Kingdoms' of Wei, Wu and Shu. A three-cornered struggle for power developed among these successor states, complicated by the presence of various peasant armies which had rebelled against the last Han emperor. There were also several 'barbarian' tribes – including Hsiung-nu from Mongolia, Hsien-pi from Manchuria in the far north-east, and Ch'iang and Ti from the borders of Tibet – which had moved into the north from the Central Asian steppes as Han authority declined. It was these barbarians who eventually brought the 'Three Kingdoms' to an end, when in the early fourth century a Hsiung-nu chief, who went by the Chinese name of Li Yuan, convinced his people that he was the true emperor by right of his descent from a Han princess. The Hsiung-nu put this claim into practice by invading north China and capturing the former capital cities of Lo-yang and Ch'ang-an, the latter being sacked in 316 amid scenes of unforgettable savagery. The floodgates were opened, and over the next century further hordes of invaders poured in from the north, establishing a series of short-lived dynasties – usually named after more prestigious Chinese predecessors – which fought each other to a standstill across the Yellow River plain. In 351 a Ti chief named Fu Chien managed to impose his rule on the whole of northern China, setting up what was known as the dynasty of the Former Ch'in. In 383 he led a huge army, which included thousands of Chinese conscripts as well as contingents of Ti, Hsiung-nu and Hsien-pi, to conquer the south, but he was ambushed at the Fei River and his regime disintegrated in the aftermath of his defeat. After this debacle no one else attempted to unify the whole of China for another two hundred years.

The Toba

Relative stability was not restored to the north until the early fifth century, when a Hsien-pi clan known as the Toba established a dynasty based at Ping-ch'eng in what is now northern Shansi Province. This regime took the title of Northern Wei, recalling the Warring States kingdom of Wei which had once held sway over the same region. Their success was due to a policy of integrating the steppe warriors and the local Chinese, and harnessing the skills of both in the service of the state. Nomad cavalry still supplied the core of the army, but Chinese infantry were employed to garrison fortified cities, and Chinese scholars to help administer them. Local officials were given responsibility for collecting taxes and mustering troops. The Northern Wei began to resemble a native Chinese dynasty, and like the Chinese they became increasingly preoccupied with the threat from other 'barbarians' beyond the frontiers. In 429 they despatched an expedition which advanced across the steppes as far as the T'ien Shan Mountains, defeating a nomadic tribe known as the Juan-juan and driving them westwards. The Juan-juan are often thought to have been the same people as the Avars who arrived on the eastern borders of Europe soon afterwards, just as the Hsiung-nu are sometimes equated with the Huns, though the connection between east and west is by no means certain in either case. This victory was followed by the establishment of six fortresses along the edge of the steppe, garrisoned by Toba cavalry and designed to prevent invaders gaining access to food and water supplies after their crossing of the Gobi Desert further north. In 493 the Northern Wei Emperor Hsiao-wen-ti moved his capital and many of his Toba subjects south to Lo-yang, which had never recovered from its destruction by the Hsiung-nu in 311, and restored it at great expense to its former glory. However not all of the Toba elite supported this further move towards sinicisation, and the corrupt regime of Yuan Yi, who seized power after a coup in 520, further undermined confidence in the government in Lo-yang. In 523 the troops on the northern frontier rebelled against a commander who had been depriving them of rations while hoarding the grain for his own profit, leading to a general uprising which became known as the 'Revolt of the Six Garrisons'.

The rebels were eventually defeated with the aid of the Ehrchu, a tribe of Central Asian origin which had settled in the borderlands of the north-west, and whose armoured cavalry won a spectacular victory against enormous odds at Yeh on the lower reaches of the Yellow River in 528. Their leader, Ehrchu Jung, married his daughter to the Emperor Hsiao-chuang-ti and seems to have aspired to take the throne for himself, but was forestalled when in the autumn of 530 Hsiao-chuang-ti summoned him to the palace and assassinated him with his own hand. Jung's followers retaliated by storming the city and murdering the emperor, whose last prayer to the Buddha is said to have been a plea not to be punished by being reborn as a monarch again. The Ehrchu were finally suppressed two years later, but the Wei state had been severely weakened by the troubles. Lo-yang had suffered further in 529 when an expeditionary force from the southern kingdom of Liang, led by a tactical genius named Ch'en Ch'ing-chih, had managed to capture the city after a stunning series of victories against the odds, and installed a puppet emperor. Ch'en had been sent by the Liang Emperor Wu-ti with only 7,000 men, apparently in the hope of taking advantage of the divisions in the Wei state, but by the time he arrived the 'Six Garrisons' revolt had been suppressed and Ehrchu Jung was back in command of a united army numbering several hundred thousand men. What was more the Wei soldiers were mainly cavalry, but horses were always in short supply in the southern states, and it is likely that most of Ch'en's men were on foot. Nevertheless he outmanoeuvred Jung, luring him south by attacking a number of frontier towns, and then slipping past him to descend on the undefended capital at Lo-yang. The southerners seized the city and held it for two months, but were unable to gain significant support from disaffected elements in the Wei Empire, and their own emperor unaccountably failed to reinforce them. Ehrchu Jung eventually retook Lo-yang, but Ch'en managed to break out and retreat southwards, though suffering heavy losses to the Wei cavalry in the pursuit.

Ch'en was soon driven out, but the prestige of the Wei dynasty never fully recovered from this setback, and in 534 quarrelling warlords split the empire into two parts. The Eastern Wei, led by a general named Kao Huan, the conqueror of the Ehrchu, controlled the region around the former capital at Lo-yang, while Ch'ang-an and the 'Land Within the Passes' became the territory of the Western Wei. Unfortunately for the latter, however, their base was no longer the fertile breadbasket which had fed the armies of the Chou, Ch'in and Han, but had become increasingly impoverished by war and the exhaustion of the soil. Enmity between the two states was guaranteed by the fact that both harboured princes of the Toba royal house who continued to describe themselves as the sole ruler of the old Northern Wei empire. Fearing that Lo-yang was too close to enemy territory for safety, Kao moved his headquarters east to Yeh, leaving the former capital to fall once again into ruins. Nevertheless the stretch of the middle Yellow River where Lo-yang was situated remained strategically valuable to both sides, and over the next few years the territory between the city and the passes leading into the Western Wei heartland became one of the most fought-over places in Chinese history.

With Kao Huan's power base encompassing the whole of the prosperous middle and lower reaches of the Yellow River, and his western rivals confined to the barren uplands 'within the passes', the outcome of the ensuing power struggle must have seemed inevitable. What was more, Kao was a skilled statesman who attempted with some success to reconcile the Hsien-pi military aristocracy with the native Chinese population. According to one account he would remind the Hsien-pi that the Chinese were their slaves, who supplied them with food and clothing and were therefore far too useful to be oppressed and alienated. At the same time he would tell the Chinese that the 'barbarians' were valuable servants to them, as they bore arms and protected them from invaders in return for a modest payment in grain and cloth. But the military disparity between the two new states was far less than it seemed. One reason was that the westerners were on the whole more conservative, retaining the warlike nature of their Toba ancestors, and less inclined to divert their energies into matters like religion or trade. Another was the personality of their leader, for the power behind the throne of the Western Wei was one of the most famous war leaders in Chinese history, a man named Yu-wen T'ai. He was born in 507 into an old Hsien-pi noble family, and in 534 he held the title of Duke of An-ting, controlling large estates near Ch'ang-an. It was there that the Toba Emperor Hsiao-wu sought asylum after the disintegration of his empire, and there also that he died, allegedly from poison, in the following year. Yu-wen T'ai always protested his loyalty to the old Wei dynasty, but he was widely suspected of organising Hsiao-wu's demise, especially when one of his cousins subsequently took the throne under the name of Emperor Wen of the Western Wei.

Armour and Stirrups: Chinese Heavy Cavalry of the Fourth to Sixth Centuries AD

By the end of the third century BC, if not earlier, the civilisations of the Middle East and the Eastern Mediterranean had begun to develop heavily armoured shock cavalry, armed with lances and riding armoured horses, and designed to overthrow the enemy by the sheer weight of their close order charge. The idea of such cavalry was not new even then of course. By around 400 BC some Persian nobles were already equipping their horses with limited protection for the chest and forehead. Alexander the Great's Macedonian Companions had charged to victory against the Persians using long lances in the 330s, but they had still possessed only light body armour for the riders, and relied mainly on speed and dash – the equivalent of Napoleon's lancers, perhaps, rather than his cuirassiers. But by the time of the Battle of Panion in 200 BC Alexander's successors were fielding units of 'kataphraktoi' or cataphracts, which Polybius describes as having 'men and horses completely armoured'. Like most innovations in the art of cavalry warfare, this one is generally believed to have originated in Central Asia – specifically among the Parthians, who established their empire in Iran around 250 BC. In that case the Chinese, who as we have seen were in contact with Parthia during the Eastern Han period, must have been familiar with their 'kataphraktoi', who though not the most numerous component of the army, were surely the most spectacular. And yet the cavalry of the Han dynasty – even those intended to charge into hand-to-hand combat – continued to wear no more than a helmet and a light 'liang-tang' corselet, and to ride on unprotected horses. At first Chinese horses, like the steppe ponies from which they were descended, were probably too small to carry the weight of extra armour, but after the introduction of the 'Heavenly Horses' from Ferghana at the end of the second century BC there seems to have been no reason to prevent the Chinese developing their own fully armoured 'cataphract' cavalry arm. In his study of the stirrup in China, Albert Dien suggests that progress with heavily burdened horsemen was delayed because the main opposition for the Han cavalry was provided by the lightly equipped mounted archers of the Hsiung-nu, against whom heavy cavalry would have been ineffective because of their reduced mobility. However the Parthians had developed tactics for employing mixed forces of both types to great effect against horse-archers, and in any case it appears that the steppe tribes were already developing their own heavy cavalry arm.

The first sign that Chinese cavalry were at last catching up with the west comes from a quotation attributed to Ts'ao Ts'ao, the hero of the Three Kingdoms era, who died in AD 220 (Dien, 1987). Ts'ao boasted that he had defeated his enemies despite serious deficiencies in the equipment of his own soldiers, who possessed only ten sets of horse armour compared to 300. Ts'ao Chu, writing around 226, also refers to a type of protection for horses known as 'ma-k'ai i-ling'. The appearance of armoured horses might explain why charging cavalry become more prominent in battle accounts of the Three Kingdoms, despite their limited numbers, but Dien points out that the only archaeological evidence that is even roughly contemporary is a tomb figurine dated to 302, which depicts a horse wearing no more than a simple strip of what appears to be lamellar armour across the chest. Thus at the beginning of the fourth century AD Chinese horse armour was at about the same stage of development as that of the Persians had been 700 years earlier. This situation changed drastically over the next few decades. The catastrophic barbarian invasions which began with the sack of Lo-yang in 311 brought hordes of Hsiung-nu and Hsien-pi horsemen into China, and at least some among the tribal elites rode armoured horses. In fact there is some evidence that complete cataphract-style armour for man and horse may have been invented independently in the east by the Hsien-pi or their Korean neighbours. The Hsiung-nu are described as capturing large numbers of horse armours from their Hsien-pi rivals on two occasions in the early fourth century: in 312, when 5,000 equipments were taken at the breaking of a siege of Lo-yang by Shih Lo, and in 316 when the same chief took another 10,000 in a successful ambush. The earliest known depiction of an Oriental equivalent of the 'kataphraktoi', with man and horse fully armoured, comes from the tomb of Tung Shou, a Chinese officer buried in Korea in 357. It appears from the sometimes somewhat crude pictorial representations of the era that the horse armour, like that of the riders, consisted of laced lamellar plates made either of metal or of leather. Shields seem never to have been very popular with Oriental cavalrymen, and these cataphracts continued to be depicted without them.

From the end of the fourth century onwards such troops become fairly common in art from all over China, including places like Yunnan in the far south-west, where the nomad armies never penetrated. The implication is that by this time it was not only the invading barbarians and their allies in the north who employed heavy cavalry, but that the native Chinese kingdoms in the south had also adopted it. But at first the introduction of new cavalry equipment does not seem to have led to a revolution in tactics. Western cataphracts apparently advanced at a walk or trot in close order, depending on their long lances to deter any attempt by more mobile opponents to break into their formation. On the other hand, as Dien complains, in Chinese sources we generally hear of the exploits of individual champions rather than the manoeuvres of formed bodies. A classic example was Ch'en An, who was killed in 323 while wielding a sword in one hand and a lance in the other, but who also carried a bow with which he shot arrows at his enemies as they closed in. In fact bows seem to have been standard equipment for even the most heavily armed Chinese horsemen – again in contrast to the practice in Parthia and Europe, where the roles of the cataphracts and the lighter mounted archers were usually kept separate. This implies that the eastern cavalrymen were more mobile, and probably habitually fought in looser

formations to facilitate skirmishing with their bows. One fourth-century
Hsien-pi army, however, seems to have been an exception. Five thousand
armoured mounted archers from the Mu-jung clan were reportedly
chained together in a square to resist the charge of their Hsiung-nu
counterparts. The Hsiung-nu came on with lances and halberds – their
leader carrying a lance in his left hand, and a halberd in his right – and
succeeded in killing 300 of the defenders, but they were unable to break
the square and were eventually defeated. It is of course possible that the
chains were simply a metaphor for a close-packed, disciplined formation,
but they may have been a desperate improvisation by a commander who
had decided, for whatever reason, to stand on the defensive, and needed
to prevent the less determined among his troopers from giving way in
this unfamiliar role. But for cavalry to deliberately sacrifice its mobility
in this way goes against all the traditional tenets of mounted warfare, and
despite its success on this occasion the experiment was apparently not
repeated.

A development which seems to have been contemporary with the
appearance of horse armour was the invention of the stirrup, which
also first appeared early in the fourth century and became widespread
over the next century or so. There has been a great deal of controversy
over the role of stirrups in military history, with some writers claiming
that cavalry could not charge home and fight hand-to-hand effectively
without them (see the discussion in Dien). In reality horsemen in both
east and west had done so for centuries before the stirrup appeared, often
gaining support instead from a well-designed saddle. However, stirrups
may well have been useful for men attempting the athletic Chinese style
of fighting – often with both hands occupied with weapons – while
wearing heavy armour. Another school of thought points to the benefits
of the additional stability provided by stirrups when shooting powerful
bows from horseback (Karasulas), but the very earliest evidence cited in
support of this theory comes from the western steppes around the first
century AD, long after the Hsiung-nu had built their empire on the skills
of their mounted archers.

Whatever the factors that lay behind it may have been, there does
seem to have been a qualitative change in cavalry warfare at some time
in the late fifth or early sixth centuries, because in the revolt of the Six

Garrisons and the wars of the Eastern and Western Wei we hear for the first time of battles being decided by true massed charges. In the Official History of the Wei dynasty there survives a detailed account of Ehrchu Jung's victory at Yeh, which gives the distinct impression that this battle saw the introduction of a new style of fighting (Jenner). An army of rebels from the Six Garrisons, led by Ko Jung and said to have been a million strong, advanced up the Yellow River valley from the east in the direction of Lo-yang. These northern frontier troops were predominantly, if not exclusively, armoured cavalry, and most of them must have been veterans of numerous wars against the steppe tribes. Nevertheless Ehrchu Jung decided not to rely on the regular Wei army based at Lo-yang, but instead to march to meet the enemy with only 7,000 riders from his own tribe. Clearly he intended to rely on surprise and mobility rather than numbers, and there are indications that he had trained his men in a devastating new tactic. This would explain both his confidence and his reluctance to employ additional troops, who had presumably not been specially trained and so could not be relied upon to adhere to the plan. We are told that each Ehrchu trooper was supplied with a weapon known as a 'shen-pang', or 'miraculous cudgel', which was to be held beside the horse's flank until the last moment, then used in close combat instead of the usual swords. Jung's men advanced as a single compact body against one section of the enemy line and broke through it. They then rallied in their rear and charged the rebels again from behind before they could turn their clumsy formation to face the new threat. Ko Jung was taken prisoner, and most of his men then surrendered. The 'shen-pang' is not described in detail, but it can hardly have involved some new and decisive technology. Although charging cavalry continued to be a decisive factor in Chinese warfare for many centuries, the 'shen-pang' is not heard of again, which suggests that its real advantage was that of surprise. In other words, it was a familiar piece of equipment but used in a new way. Understandably it has been suggested that the name refers to a lance which was couched like that of a European medieval knight – held firmly under the arm and propelled by the momentum of the horse, rather than being wielded overarm in one or both hands as is shown in earlier Chinese art. This cannot be confirmed from contemporary artistic representations or written sources, but it would explain the effectiveness of the Ehrchu charge. On the other hand the use of the lance from horseback is not a skill which can be taught quickly, and an inexperienced lancer is relatively easy prey for a sword-armed opponent, as was evident when the lance was reintroduced into Western Europe during the Napoleonic Wars. Perhaps we should take the 'cudgel' description more literally, and reconstruct it as a type of mace. The reason for holding the weapon down alongside the horse would then be to conceal it from the enemy until the last moment, preventing him from devising countermeasures, and hopefully disconcerting him by the unexpected sight of thousands of iron clubs flashing into action just before the ranks closed. In any case the couched lance – if used skilfully – and the hypothetical mace would have had similar advantages over swords or halberds; they could be wielded more effectively in close order, allowing the Ehrchu to maintain the density of their formation, and they would remove the temptation to stop and collect heads. Ever since the Warring States period Chinese soldiers had been encouraged to cut off the heads of their victims as proof of their success, and social status and even promotion still often depended on obtaining such trophies, but a small group of men fighting against great odds could not afford to stop and disperse for such a purpose until the enemy was conclusively defeated. But whatever the precise nature of the weapons and tactics employed, heavy cavalry armed for close combat had now become the cutting edge of northern Chinese armies, as the conflict between the two rival Wei regimes was to illustrate.

Although cavalry was now the principal offensive arm, at least of the northern 'barbarian' armies, most regimes continued to raise infantry from among the Chinese and non-Chinese populations. The Northern Wei established a system known as the 'Three Leaders', under which their Chinese subjects were organised for recruitment purposes. Tomb figures of this period are often depicted on foot and carrying either bows or swords and shields, and the facial features and full beards of some of them have led to speculation that they are intended to depict men of Central Asian origin rather than Chinese. They are associated with a distinctive style of armour which represents the first major development in Chinese armour since the Warring States. Known as 'cord and plaque', it is clearly an improved version of the Han 'liang-tang', with the front and back plates made of solid metal or leather and reinforced by extra plaques to provide further protection for the chest and stomach. A system of cords on the outside of the armour is sometimes interpreted as holding the plaques in place (Dien, 1981), but this would not be a very secure method of fastening heavy pieces of armour, and it seems more likely that the function of the cords was to distribute some of the weight from the wearer's shoulders to the waist. Whether the tomb figures are actually evidence for armoured infantry is uncertain. Their function was to act as guardians for deceased noblemen, and so it would be natural to depict them as they would appear when on guard duty, when they would be dismounted and equipped with shields like infantrymen. The 'cord and plaque' armour looks elaborate and expensive as well as heavy, and it would not be surprising if at least some of its wearers belonged to the elite who served on the battlefield as heavy cavalry.

The Sha-yuan Campaign

The opening move in the deadly struggle between the two successor states was launched by the Eastern Wei. In the spring of 537 Kao Huan despatched two armies west from Lo-yang under the command of Tou T'ai and Kao Ao-ts'ao. The plan was apparently for the latter to mount a feint attack to lure Yu-wen T'ai out of the T'ong Pass so that Tou T'ai could outflank him and seize the pass, thus cutting his lines of communication. However the westerners turned the tables by making public preparations to withdraw westwards and abandon Ch'ang-an, enticing Tou to push hastily over the mountains with the aim of seizing the city. Yu-wen T'ai then turned back eastwards by forced marches and surprised Tou at Hsiao-kuan, inflicting a defeat and forcing him to retreat. Meanwhile Kao Ao-ts'ao's army was also closing in. He crossed the T'ong Pass and advanced as far as Wei-ch'u, where he ran into an ambush set by the western general Li Pi. Li concealed troops on both sides of the road where it ran through a marsh, hidden in the extensive reedbeds, and then sent forward a small detachment of cavalry which skirmished with the head of the enemy column, then fell back, luring it into the trap. As the disordered easterners retreated over the pass, Yu-wen T'ai brought up his cavalry and pursued them. But on the far side of the mountains he encountered the main eastern army, consisting allegedly of 200,000 men in two huge columns commanded by Kao Huan himself. It was now the turn of the westerners to retreat. Kao Huan stormed through the T'ong Pass and emerged onto the open plain with his overwhelmingly superior army at Sha-yuan, just inside the stronghold of his enemy. But Yu-wen T'ai had concealed 10,000 heavy cavalry on his side of the pass, deployed parallel to the enemy's line of march. It is not clear whether he had planned this move from the beginning, and his own foray across the mountains was just another decoy, or whether he had hastily improvised the trap in response to Kao Huan's unexpected thrust, but the result was the same. By the time he was aware of the western cavalry thundering down on his flank, it was far too late for Kao to deploy to meet them. Six thousand easterners are said to have been killed in the first onslaught, and another 70,000 were taken prisoner as they fled in panic back towards the pass. Like Yeh nine years earlier, Sha-yuan was surely another victory for massed heavy cavalry, charging in coherent formation into hand-to-hand combat. No other tactic seems able to explain the speed and decisiveness with which their far more numerous opponents were overthrown.

The Struggle for Lo-yang

Yu-wen T'ai's men were less successful at following up their victory, however. Towards the end of 537 an expedition under Tu-ku Hsin and Wei Hsiao-k'uan occupied Lo-yang, but in the following spring Tu-ku Hsin was besieged there by a fresh eastern army led by Kao Ao-ts'ao and Hou Ching. Yu-wen T'ai, accompanied by the Emperor Wen in person, marched to raise the siege. This time the easterners used his own tactics against him, first falling back, then turning to strike hard at their pursuers. Yu-wen was leading the pursuit near Ho-ch'iao when his horse was wounded by an arrow and threw him. Disguising himself as an ordinary trooper in order to avoid capture, he somehow got back to his camp and organised a counterattack, during which his enemy Kao Ao-ts'ao was killed. An incident recounted in the 'Chou Shu', the Official History of the Northern Chou dynasty, gives a vivid picture of the fighting during these battles. When the easterners advanced, a Western Wei general named Ts'ai Yu found himself caught between the opposing armies with a small band of followers. Despite the remonstrances of his companions he dismounted, exclaiming 'The Chancellor (ie. Yu-wen

T'ai) raised me like a son. How can I think of my own fate today?' Then he charged into the enemy ranks at the head of only ten of his men, all of whom were presumably on foot. They killed many of the easterners in desperate hand-to-hand fighting, but were soon surrounded by a ring of enemies ten men deep. Believing him to be in a hopeless situation the eastern soldiers called on Ts'ai Yu to surrender, offering him wealth and honours in recognition of his courage. But Ts'ai cursed them, remarking scornfully that all he had to do to attain the rank of duke was to take their heads back to Yu-wen T'ai. He then drew his bow and defied them to take him, but they were afraid to face his arrows and hung back. Then they called up a champion, who was wearing exceptionally heavy armour and carrying a long sword. This man advanced towards Ts'ai, and when he was thirty paces away the westerners urged their leader to shoot, but he continued to hold his fire. Realising that he would not have time to shoot more than once, he answered 'Our life rides on one arrow – how can I shoot it in vain?' When the enemy was only ten paces distant, he finally loosed the arrow. It struck the easterner in the face, where he was unprotected by armour, and Ts'ai ran up and finished him off with a lance. No doubt the reason for shooting at such a perilously short distance was less the difficulty of hitting the target at longer ranges, than the necessity for a very short flight time in order to prevent the victim dodging or blocking the arrow. The fight continued for a while longer and one of the western fighters was killed, but their enemies became increasingly demoralised and eventually fell back. Ts'ai Yu then led his men slowly back to friendly lines. Dien comments that 'literary convention may have recast this conflict into terms of individual combat, for it would make no sense to send a single cavalryman on such a mission.' However it seems equally likely that Ts'ai and his little party were trapped accidentally in this desperate situation when the easterners first attacked, and that his courage and presence of mind saved their lives. Personal skill at arms was always a prime requisite for a Chinese commander, and battle accounts from this period show that even officers as eminent as Yu-wen T'ai himself continued to risk death or capture by leading their cavalry from the front.

But despite the bravery and coolness of men like Ts'ai Yu, the westerners were once again forced to fall back later that day, when the enemy rallied and returned to the fray in overwhelming force. Eastern

Wei sources subsequently claimed to have killed tens of thousands of them in the bitter fighting at Ho-ch'iao. Yu-wen T'ai reluctantly ordered a general retreat back across the passes, which turned into a race for survival when news came in that the city of Hong-nong, which lay on their line of retreat, had fallen into enemy hands. Regrettably we have no details of how Yu-wen extricated himself from the trap, but the western army eventually fought its way back to Ch'ang-an. There the survivors discovered that the prisoners taken at Sha-yuan had learned of their captors' discomfiture and rebelled, causing extensive damage. They were suppressed after further fighting, but by now both sides were exhausted, and neither undertook any major initiatives for the next few years.

Then in 542 the easterners attacked Yu-pi, on the east bank of the Yellow River in present-day Shansi, which was held for the Western Wei by Tu-ku Hsin's colleague from the Lo-yang campaign of 537, Wei Hsiao-k'uan. The first attempt at besieging the city had to be abandoned after only nine days, when a blizzard struck the easterners encamped on the open plain and many of them died of exposure. Kao Huan returned shortly afterwards, however, with a larger army which surrounded Yu-pi and cut it off from the river and its water supply. Kao then built a huge mound of earth and wood to overlook the walls on the south side of the city, but Wei Hsiao-k'uan responded by building the walls and towers higher. Then the besiegers dug tunnels underneath the walls, but Wei dealt with these by digging his own intersecting tunnels and setting fire to them. The fire spread into the enemy's excavations and killed many of their troops. Battering rams deployed against the gates were also destroyed by fire. Finally, after fifty days of siege operations, during which Wei had countered every move he could think of, Kao lifted the siege and retired.

Then early in 543 Yu-wen T'ai was once again lured out of his stronghold by the promise of gains in the east. Kao Chung-mi, the governor of the Eastern Wei district of Northern Yu (in what is now Henan Province), decided to change sides and deliver his territory to the westerners. An army set out from Ch'ang-an to link up with him and take Lo-yang, but in the Mang Mountains outside the city it encountered the main eastern force under P'eng Lo. Yu-wen T'ai attacked, but failed to break through P'eng's line. According to one account Yu-wen was temporarily cut off, and only escaped capture by offering bribes. Nevertheless he renewed the attack the following day, but was finally forced to acknowledge defeat. Yet again he managed to keep his army substantially intact, and brought it home through the T'ong Pass, abandoning Kao Chung-mi to his fate.

The End of the Wei

Yu-wen is said to have lost 400 officers and 60,000 men in this disastrous campaign. He was so demoralised that he offered his resignation, but the Emperor Wen refused to accept it. Nevertheless the Western Wei had to abandon any hope of reuniting the former Wei empire by force. When in 547 another eastern general, Hou Ching, offered to defect, only a small flying column was sent east to make contact with him. Yu-wen instructed Hou to leave his own district and bring his troops to Ch'ang-an to join up with the western army, but he refused. Hou instead accepted an invitation to join the Liang in the south, perhaps because the journey was less risky, but then changed sides again and treacherously sacked the Liang capital at Chien-k'ang. This set off a chain of events which led to the disintegration of the Liang, and in 552 the ruler of the western portion of the state, in what is now Szechwan, accepted the Western Wei emperor as his overlord. At this point, with Yu-wen T'ai's regime apparently at the pinnacle of its success, both of the Wei states underwent a change of dynasty, being replaced by the Northern Chou in the west and the Northern Ch'i in the east. But these upheavals were mere palace coups rather than full-scale rebellions, and were carried out with little bloodshed. If the ruling families had changed, the same mixed Chinese and Hsien-pi military aristocracies continued to hold power on both sides of the T'ong Pass. In fact Yu-wen T'ai remained in office under the Northern Chou until his death in 556, and it seems certain that his influence helped to determine the direction that the new regime would take.

The Northern Ch'i, the successor to the Eastern Wei, was a rich but unmilitary society which spent most of its resources on maintaining Buddhist temples, and relied mainly on building long walls to secure its frontiers. By contrast the Northern Chou taxed the temples and the monks to fund a large mobile army, and concentrated on recruiting native Chinese soldiers to augment its Toba cavalry. In 577 it finally realised Yu-wen T'ai's ambition by destroying the Northern Ch'i. After the fall of the Liang most of the southern half of China had already been reduced to vassal status by the Western Wei and its successor, and by the 570s only the state of Ch'en on the lower Yangtze maintained its independence. In 577 Ch'en sent a contingent to fight alongside the Northern Chou, but their only reward was to be driven out of the north in the aftermath of the Chou victory. The North China Plain was now under unified control for the first time since 534. As the sixth century approached its end, the momentum towards reunification of the empire continued to gather pace. In 581 the Northern Chou was overthrown in its turn, this time by a coup led by an official of native Chinese descent, Yang Chien. Yang soon completed the task of unification by destroying Ch'en, and by 589 he was the undisputed master of the whole of China, bringing to an end three centuries of political fragmentation.

Chapter Seven

The Battle of Ssu-Shui, AD 621

'Against those skilled in attack, the enemy does not know where to defend;
against the experts in defence, the enemy does not know where to attack.'
Sun Tzu.

Failed Unification: The Sui Dynasty

Styling himself Wen-ti, first emperor of the Sui dynasty, Yang Chien embarked on an ambitious plan of massive public works and territorial expansion. No doubt he believed that he now had an opportunity to equal or even surpass the great achievements of the Han, but after the long series of wars and invasions the empire was not yet strong enough to bear the burden. It was Wen-ti who built the famous Grand Canal which enabled regular supplies of rice to be brought north from the Yangtze region, but in the process he strained the imperial finances and earned the hatred of the many thousands who were forced to contribute labour for the scheme. He rebuilt many of the defensive fortifications in the north-west, which the nomad dynasties had allowed to deteriorate, and kept the 'barbarians' at bay for a while by astute diplomacy, but a campaign in Champa, beyond the south-eastern frontier, led to heavy losses from disease for no lasting gain. Wen-ti's successor Yang-ti reoccupied the Tarim Basin in the north-west, but was then lured into a disastrous war against the Korean kingdom of Koguryo. In four successive years, beginning in 612, Yang-ti sent huge conscript armies into Korea. The largest of these was said to have numbered as many as a million men, and the emperor must surely have thought that a force of this size would overawe all resistance. But each time the people of Koguryo succeeded in turning the climate and terrain against them. As was said of Spain in the Napoleonic Wars, the mountains of Korea were country in which a small army would be defeated and a large army would

A cavalryman wielding a lance overhead in both hands, as depicted in a tomb mural from Korea, dating from the Koguryo period (fourth to seventh centuries AD). This rather crude figure clearly depicts the complete lamellar armour for both man and horse which came into use in China during the fourth century. Note also what appear to be feather plumes worn by both horse and rider, and the longer plume protruding from the horse's back behind the saddle. These accoutrements are frequently depicted in Chinese art, and probably represent an arrangement of horsehair and feathers, designed to rustle in the wind like the wings of a seventeenth century Polish winged hussar with the aim of intimidating an opponent and alarming his mount.

starve. The defenders held up the Chinese with a chain of fortifications, harassed their supply lines, and waited until autumn rains and winter snows closed the mountain passes behind them.

The Revolt of Li Yuan

The cumulative Chinese losses were enormous, and the survivors returned home demoralised. By 617 the Sui was losing its grip on power, and the empire was once again plunged into chaos as competing warlords scrambled for the throne. The most eminent of these men was Li Yuan, the Duke of T'ang, who was the garrison commander at Chin-yang, the town on the north-western frontier which had once been the headquarters of Ehrchu Jung. For the career of Li and his sons we are indebted to the account of Ssu-ma Kuang, a descendant of Ssu-ma Ch'ien, who wrote under the Sung dynasty. Li Yuan's grandfather had been a minister of the Western Wei, and it appears that he was partly descended from Hsien-pi 'barbarians' who had settled in the area. Thanks to this family background, he enjoyed good relations with the steppe tribes, including a new power which had arisen during the sixth century, the T'u-Chueh or Turks. The impression gained from outside sources is that the Turks were new arrivals on the Central Asian steppe, but it is likely that they were derived from a coalition of Hsiung-nu, Juan-juan and other elements who had rebelled against their Juan-juan masters in the 550s. The supreme ruler or Khagan of the T'u-Chueh, who bore the Hsiung-nu name of Touman, established a short-lived state which stretched from the borders of China to the Caspian Sea, but in 582 this vast empire split into two parts, known as the Eastern and Western Turkish Khanates. As heirs of the Hsiung-nu the Turks relied on similar mounted archery tactics, but they were renowned metal workers, and many of their cavalry seem to have been better armoured than their predecessors. A minority of them employed horse armour and backed up their archery with the lance, mace and sword.

By the end of 617 it must have been obvious to all observers that the Sui could no longer command the allegiance of its subjects. The Emperor Yang-ti had retreated to the southern city of Yang-chou, leaving no fewer than nine 'rebel' armies in control of different regions of the empire. Yet Ssu-ma Kuang, no doubt following the T'ang Official History, repeats an unlikely story that Li Yuan still hesitated to abandon his allegiance to the Sui, only agreeing to make his own bid for power when coerced into doing so by his own son, Li Shih-min. The latter was the second son of his father, and at this time was about seventeen years old. His ability as a cavalry commander may already have been recognised, and along with Li Yuan's other sons he had been given a commission to raise troops for the forthcoming struggle, but it is hard to believe that he was in a position to dictate to his father on political matters. According to Ssu-ma Kuang, however, Li Shih-min urged the wavering Li Yuan to abandon Yang-ti, and was threatened with arrest for his pains. The boy then conspired with another Sui official, Liu Wen-ching, to discredit his own father in the eyes of his emperor. Emperor Yang-ti had kept a small harem in Chin-yang, where he could relax while overseeing campaigns on the northern border, and Li Shih-min arranged for some of the women to be presented as concubines to his father, but without telling him where they had come from. Once the women were safely inside Li Yuan's house the conspirators revealed the truth, adding that since the Emperor would surely have him executed for stealing 'his' concubines, he now had no choice but to take up arms on his own account.

This story is frankly preposterous. Li Yuan was an experienced commander and diplomat, and was hardly likely to allow his teenage son to manipulate him in such a crude fashion. Li Shih-min's alleged conduct violated not only military discipline, but also the powerful Chinese tradition of filial piety. And yet Li Yuan continued to trust both him and Liu Wen-ching, and to entrust them with important diplomatic and military tasks. In any case he had no reason to fear Yang-ti, who was virtually blockaded in his distant bolt hole by other rebel armies. There exists an alternative source to Ssu-ma Kuang, Wen Ta-ya's *Diary of the Founding of the Great T'ang*, which was written closer to the events in question and seems generally more plausible. According to this account it was Li Yuan himself who initiated the campaign that followed. The only logical reason for the persistence of Ssu-ma Kuang's version seems to be that it was promoted by Li Shih-min, who later deposed his own father and reigned as Emperor T'ai-tsung. In this capacity he oversaw the compilation of the Official History of the T'ang dynasty, and may have wished to be portrayed as the real founder of the regime as a way of excusing his disloyalty. This background should be borne in mind when assessing the surviving narrative of the Battle of Ssu-shui, which is heavily dependent on the same official sources.

In the summer of 617 Li Yuan led an army of 30,000 men south along the valley of the Fen River in the direction of Ch'ang-an, the former 'Western Capital' of the Sui, which was still held by forces loyal to the dynasty. On the way they captured the towns of Fen-chou and Huo-chou, bypassed P'u-chou at the mouth of the T'ong Pass, and occupied the pass unopposed. They then marched westward up the Wei River. Li Shih-min's older brother Li Chien-ch'eng was left to hold the pass with

10,000 men in case the Sui managed to mount a relief expedition, while his father and brother besieged Ch'ang-an. By this time several other rebel forces in the area had joined them, including one led by Li Yuan's daughter Li Che, who advanced on the city from the west. After a siege of five weeks Ch'ang-an fell. The population and the captured Sui ministers were treated well, and many soldiers and officials now joined the T'ang, as the new regime came to be known. Among them was Prince Yang Yu, Yang-ti's grandson, who was retained as a puppet emperor, while Li Yuan appointed himself chancellor, with the title of Prince of T'ang. By occupying the strategically secure 'Land Within the Passes' the T'ang had gained an important advantage over the rival contenders for power, but several years of hard fighting still lay ahead before their victory was assured.

Li Shih-min Takes Command

The official account continues to emphasise the part played in these campaigns by Li Shih-min, who had apparently been placed in command of the field armies while his father concentrated on organising the new imperial administration. This seems strange in view of Li Shih-min's youth, and the fact that his brother Chien-ch'eng was his senior, but an incident at the siege of Huo-chou may have persuaded their father of the younger boy's superior military talent. The Sui commander at Huo-chou, Sung Lao-sheng, was known to be brave but reckless, and it seems that the besiegers had deliberately tried to lure him out of his defences by openly laying out siege works on the plain before the walls. In an account known as the *Questions and Replies of T'ang T'ai-tsung and Li Wei-kung*, Li Shih-min – the future Emperor T'ai-tsung – himself described what happened next. The Sui troops did fall into the trap and sally out of the city, but they attacked so fiercely that Li Chien-ch'eng was knocked from his horse and his men were forced to fall back. Li Shih-min, seeing this, quickly gathered a force of elite cavalry and led it in a charge into the enemy's rear. The Sui were routed, and their commander was caught and beheaded. At this the garrison surrendered the town without further resistance.

Nevetheless if Li Shih-min's father really had appointed him commander-in-chief of the T'ang armies, he was taking a chance. The young prince may have been a bold and decisive cavalry officer, but he was still a novice in the art of strategy. This point is illustrated by an often-repeated story told by Ssu-ma Kuang, which was no doubt intended to depict his subject as a hero, but which inadvertently provides a picture of his inexperienced and impetuous youth. During the campaign of 619 against Liu Wu-chou, Li Shih-min was leading a group of cavalry ahead of the main army across the open steppe of the northern frontier. Seeing a hill which would provide a good vantage point, he took a single officer as an escort and rode to the top of it. They found the summit unoccupied, so with astonishing carelessness they dismounted and both lay down for a rest, apparently not bothering to keep a watch. But they had been seen by the enemy, and about a hundred horsemen were despatched to surround the hill and capture the young T'ang commander. He was saved from this humiliation only by chance, because his companion spotted a snake and leapt to his feet, saw enemy troopers moving below, and gave the alarm. Li Shih-min seized his bow and killed the enemy leader with his first shot, whereupon the two men mounted their horses and galloped back to their own army. Bizarrely, Li Shih-min is said to have made the same mistake two years later at the siege of Lo-yang, when he took 500 riders up onto the grave mound of a former emperor outside the city in order to observe the defences. This time he found himself surrounded by 10,000 defenders, and had to be rescued by another T'ang army which had arrived just in time. On this occasion several thousand of the enemy were killed or captured by the relieving force, which enabled the T'ang Official History to present it as a victory, but at the very least it suggests that their commander-in-chief was still suffering from a serious case of overconfidence.

Li Shih-min's first independent campaign was against a warlord named Hsueh Chu, who early in 618 advanced on Ch'ang-an from his base in Kansu in the far north-west. Li Shih-min inflicted a reverse on Hsueh Chu at Fu Feng, but allowed him to extricate his army intact while the T'ang forces marched east to deal with the garrison of P'u-chou, which was still holding out but which can hardly have presented a serious threat. Hsueh rallied, attacked again, and defeated the T'ang at the Battle of Ch'ien Shui Yuan. According to Ssu-ma Kuang's account Li Shih-min was ill at this time, and the T'ang were commanded in this battle by his deputy Liu Wen-ching, but the later T'ang sources are so consistent in avoiding any suggestion of imperfection on the part of the future emperor that we are justified in regarding this version with scepticism. The invaders then moved on Ch'ang-an, but Hsueh's untimely death obliged his successor to abandon the campaign, and when he returned in the autumn Li Shih-min was ready for him. Lured into attacking a decoy camp, he was taken in the rear by T'ang cavalry and his army destroyed. In 619 Li Shih-min moved north against Liu Wu-chou, finally catching and routing him in a seventy-mile cavalry pursuit at Squirrel Pass on the Fen River.

The Siege of Lo-yang

By this time the Sui emperor Yang-ti had been assassinated, and the competing warlords had thrown off all pretence of allegiance to the old dynasty. In 618 Li Yuan persuaded Prince Yang Yu to nominate him as his successor. Li then immediately deposed Yang Yu, and proclaimed himself Emperor Kao-tzu of the T'ang dynasty, with its capital at Ch'ang-an. But elsewhere in the empire the various factions had also begun to coalesce into larger kingdoms, one of the most formidable of which was that of the former Sui general Wang Shih-chung. In 620 Wang occupied the old 'Eastern Capital' at Lo-yang, on the Yellow River downstream of the T'ong Pass, and early in the following year Li Shih-min was sent east to besiege it. Wang responded by making an alliance with Tou Chien-te, whose 'Hsia' regime was based further east, on the lower reaches of the Yellow River. This was a prosperous region with very large reserves of manpower, and soon it was rumoured that Tou was raising a vast army to march to the relief of his ally. Li Shih-min therefore sent a detachment to block this expected move by occupying a position at Ssu-shui, about thirty miles east of Lo-yang. Here the road from the east crossed a ford near the mouth of the Ssu-shui River, which flows into the Yellow River from the south, and climbed up through a narrow ravine on the western side to the plateau beyond. The ford, and the mouth of the ravine, were commanded by the fortified town of Ssu-shui, which Wang Shih-chung had inexplicably left ungarrisoned. The position was ideally suited for defence against an enemy coming from the east, because not only was the river crossing commanded by the higher ground on the western bank, but the swift current of the Yellow River, flowing from west to east, made it easy to bring down supplies by boat from the west, and correspondingly difficult to convey them overland or against the current from the east.

At first the T'ang armies outside Lo-yang were not strong enough to commence formal siege operations, but they cut off the city's food supplies and eventually forced Wang to come out and offer battle. The encounter was fought on a range of hills known as the Pei Mang Shan, and pitted around 20,000 of Wang's men against a T'ang army which was probably larger, though exact figures are not recorded. The opponents seem to have been fairly evenly matched, however, as two T'ang cavalry charges failed to break the enemy, and at one point Li Shih-min found himself fighting for his life on foot after his horse was killed. Eventually Wang fell back into the city. Each side had lost around 7,000 men, but the T'ang were able to replace their losses more easily, and as their siege equipment came up they intensified their operations. Wang sent increasingly desperate messages to his ally pleading for help, and at last news arrived in the T'ang camp that Tou Chien-te was on the move, leading an army said to be 300,000 strong. Ssu-ma Kuang says that Li Shih-min's officers advised him to abandon the siege and retire beyond the T'ong Pass, but for once Li Shih-min's reckless overconfidence coincided with strategic wisdom. In the long term the T'ang could hardly be expected to prevail once they had allowed their two strongest enemies to join forces, but for the moment Wang Shih-ch'ung was demoralised, while the Hsia army was newly raised and commanded by a man who seems to have been cautious and indecisive by nature. The time was ripe for a bold stroke.

Armies of the Sui and T'ang

The armies which fought in these campaigns were still recruited according to the Sui system, which was in turn based on that introduced by the Western Wei under Yu-wen T'ai in the 540s. The passages in the T'ang Official History dealing with military organisation, translated

by Robert des Rotours, provide a detailed picture of the early T'ang
army, although it is probably somewhat idealised, and relates specifically
to the heyday of the dynasty in the middle of the seventh century
rather than to the chaotic struggle for power in which it was founded.
Nevertheless, in broad outline it is presumably fairly accurate for both
the successors of the Sui and the forces led by Li Yuan and Li Shih-min.
Both infantry and cavalry were provided by the 'fu-ping' militia, who
were technically conscripts, but were drawn from an elite of hereditary
military families and received thorough training when not engaged in
farming or other occupations. Many of these families were of Hsien-pi
or similar 'barbarian' origin, and they were concentrated in the vicinity
of Ch'ang-an and along the northern frontier where the external threat
was greatest. Most campaigns did not therefore involve long absences
from home, and only families with more than one son of fighting age
were normally expected to send a recruit, ensuring that they were not
impoverished by their obligations. Under these circumstances military
service was not necessarily unpopular. In fact a remark made by Li Shih-
min later in his career suggests that the conscripts were accompanied
by numerous volunteers, perhaps attracted by the prospect of loot or of
social advancement. 'When we call for ten men' he boasted, 'we get a
hundred. When we call for a hundred we get a thousand'. The troops
were organised into units known as 'fu', which could comprise between
800 and 1,200 men, and included 'wu-ch'i', or heavy cavalry, 'pu-she', or
archers on foot, and 'pu-ping', 'marching infantry'.

Later T'ang regulations imply that all troops were supposed to carry
bows, but both paintings and tomb figurines, especially from the Sui period,
often show infantry with shields, swords and spears rather than bows, and
it is probably men equipped in this manner that were differentiated by
the title 'pu-ping'. Among the Sui and some of their predecessors, heavily
armoured lancer cavalry without bows also seem to have been common,
but numerous anecdotes from Li Shih-min's career refer to the use of
bows from horseback, and it is likely that not only the T'ang but many of
their opponents had already adopted the characteristically Turkish style of
fighting, emphasising mounted archery, from their neighbours beyond the
northern frontier. Li Shih-min himself, in fact, was famous for his skill as an
archer. The bows were of the Central Asian composite type which had been

popular in China as long ago as the Shang dynasty, and were formidable weapons requiring skill and practice to draw effectively. The regulations for officer selection published in 702 suggest that a typical draw weight was around 120 pounds, comparable with the sixteenth century English longbows recovered from Henry VIII's warship the *Mary Rose*. A bow of this weight would be an extremely formidable weapon, but surprisingly the arrows mentioned in the same regulations are very light, no more than six tenths of an ounce (Ranitzsch), being made, presumably, from hollow bamboo instead of solid wood. For comparison, medieval English longbow arrows are believed to have averaged between three and four ounces. The lighter projectiles would therefore have had considerably less penetration than those used at Crecy and Agincourt, though they would have had higher velocity at short range. They may, however, have been used mainly for training, for some Chinese arrows were certainly heavier: in the early twentieth century, for example, the American archer Saxton Pope acquired a traditionally made Chinese composite bow with an associated arrow which weighed four ounces – though Pope was unable to establish the draw weight of this weapon, as neither he nor anyone of his acquaintance could draw it!

Some cavalrymen depicted in art are unarmoured and presumably fought as highly mobile skirmishers, but most seem to have worn iron or leather body armour and helmets, and possibly ridden armoured horses as well. 'Cord and plaque' style armour continues to appear on tomb figures from the Sui and T'ang periods, but the T'ang appear to have preferred long lamellar sleeved coats of Central Asian type. T'ang cavalry continued to carry lances and swords in addition to their bows, and so would have been equally effective in the charge as when fighting from a distance. The 702 regulations required officer candidates to perform a difficult exercise in which they had to knock a small piece of wood off the head of a dummy with an eighteen foot lance at full gallop, without touching the dummy itself. The story of the Battle of Ssu-shui certainly suggests that Li Shih-min's troopers could skirmish and fight hand-to-hand with equal facility, and this flexibility may have been an important factor in his victory. The crossbow, once regarded as the most effective weapon of the Han infantry, seems never to have been popular with T'ang armies, no doubt because of the difficulty of stopping heavy cavalry due to its slow rate of fire. A later source claims that T'ang crossbowmen had to be provided with halberds for self-defence, and that once the enemy got to close quarters they would generally prefer to throw away their crossbows and fight hand-to-hand.

The Battle of Ssu-shui

Leaving the main T'ang army to continue the siege of Lo-yang under the command of his younger brother Li Yuan-chi, Shih-min took a force of only 3,500 picked cavalrymen and rode east to Ssu-shui to face an enemy of perhaps 300,000 men. There he was joined by the garrison which had already been installed in the town, bringing his total strength to around 10,000. Tou Chien-te was camped about seven miles further east, having failed to secure the river crossing in advance of his main body. It seems that the young T'ang general already had good intelligence about the personality of his opponent, because he immediately devised a plan to gain the moral ascendancy. First he sent 500 of his heavy cavalry across the Ssu-shui River to take up an ambush position in a defile, then he personally led a small mounted party onto the plateau beyond. There they encountered a Hsia cavalry patrol, which at first mistook them for friends; it seems likely that Tou's intelligence had failed him completely, and that he had no idea that there were T'ang troops in the vicinity. Li Shih-min, however, soon disillusioned them. He shot an arrow into the enemy officer, and announced to his men in a loud voice 'I am Li Shih-min!' The Hsia survivors galloped away, and soon afterwards a group of several thousand horsemen was seen approaching from the direction of the Hsia camp. The T'ang in their turn fled, leading their pursuers straight into Li Shih-min's ambush. Strung out and with their horses tired from the headlong ride, the Hsia were routed, leaving 300 dead and prisoners behind. The T'ang cavalry were equally successful in a series of skirmishes along the river, and the Hsia and their commander seem to have been completely unnerved. What was more, the failure of his own cavalry prevented Tou from gaining an accurate idea of the strength of the T'ang forces on the west bank. It is hard to believe that he would not have pressed on if he had known that he outnumbered the enemy by as much as thirty to one, but instead, after a feeble probing attack against the town which was easily repulsed, he set up a fortified camp on the eastern shore and remained on the defensive for several weeks.

This of course played right into the hands of the T'ang, who needed only to hold until Lo-yang had fallen and their main body arrived to reinforce them. But messengers from Wang Shih-chung were still arriving in the Hsia camp – presumably by river – begging Tou to attack. A council of war was held, at which the Hsia generals proposed bypassing the Ssu-shui position by crossing the Yellow River and advancing west along the north bank. But Wang's ambassadors argued that this would take too long, as Lo-yang was starving and could not resist much longer. Tou agreed and dismissed the plan, but still seemed reluctant to adopt the only possible alternative – a frontal attack across the river and into the hills beyond, where he was certain to be ambushed once again. It appears that the outcome of this council was reported to Li Shih-min by spies, because he now tried to encourage Tou to attack by pretending to weaken the defence. He sent 1,000 grooms and servants with spare horses across to the opposite shore of the Yellow River, as if to contest the expected crossing, then secretly brought them back by night. Tou Chien-te seems to have fallen for this trick, because finally, one hot day in the early summer of 621, he led his forces out of their camp and deployed them along the east bank of the Ssu-Shui River. Unfortunately we are not told the relative proportions of infantry and cavalry, but if there were anywhere near 300,000 men in the field, the great majority must have been poorly equipped footsoldiers. So enormous was Tou's army that it stretched for seven miles, but as the only practicable crossing was the ford opposite the town, most of these troops could have played little part in an assault. Perhaps the intention was to overawe the defenders by a show of strength, but Li Shih-min was not so easily intimidated.

Tou opened the battle by sending 300 Hsia cavalry across the ford to skirmish with their opposite numbers, and perhaps provoke them into charging out from their secure position to fight in the open plain. Li Shih-min sent a contingent of his own horsemen to meet them, and for a while the two sides skirmished indecisively, shooting from a distance but inflicting few casualties. At this point Ssu-ma Kuang describes an incident which illustrates the devotion which Li Shih-min must have inspired in his officers. The T'ang commander noticed that one of the Hsia troopers was riding an exceptionally fine horse, and remarked on it to Yu-ch'ih Ch'ing-te, one of the officers on his staff. Yu-ch'ih and two other men instantly rode out from the T'ang lines, overtook the enemy cavalryman and seized his horse by the bridle. The three then galloped back and presented the animal to Li Shih-min, complete with its rider, who seems to have been so astonished that he put up no resistance. The cavalry battle went on for some time, while the bulk of the T'ang army rested, ate and drank in their positions around the town. Meanwhile the Hsia soldiers stood under arms in the sun, only yards from the river, but forbidden to break ranks and drink. Eventually, around midday, they started to drift away from their units in search of food and water. Tou Chien-te, no doubt convinced that the enemy were not going to advance that day, had retired to his tent for another conference with his senior officers.

From his elevated command post on the west bank, Li Shih-min could observe the condition of the Hsia army, and he decided to order a probing attack to see whether they were still capable of responding. A Hsien-pi officer named Yu-wen Shih-chi was sent across the river with a small unit of cavalry, with orders to fall back if the enemy opposite tried to counterattack, but to charge them if they wavered. As the T'ang cavalry advanced, the Hsia foragers down by the river ran to rejoin their units, spreading confusion in their ranks. Shouting 'Now we can attack!' Li Shih-min led the rest of his army over the river and charged into the enemy. By now Tou and his officers were desperately trying to restore control over their scattered forces, but it was too late. The huge Hsia army did not crumble straight away, and there were hours of hard fighting still to come, but the initiative was now with the T'ang. It seems from Ssu-ma Kuang's account that although the Hsia troops stood firm and resisted numerous charges by the T'ang cavalry, they did not attempt to counterattack, or to bring their numerical superiority into play by manoeuvring against the enemy's flanks. Perhaps the very length of their line worked against them, and the officers in command of the units on the wings were unable to reach them in time to give orders. Perhaps their inexperienced soldiers and junior officers were incapable of acting on their own initiative, and were only too glad to stay out of a losing battle as long as they could. Tou is not described as exercising any further command functions, and may have lost his nerve. Whatever the reason, the Hsia units stayed on the defensive while the more mobile T'ang cavalry battered them into submission during the course of the long, hot afternoon.

The initial T'ang onslaught drove the enemy in the centre back as far as the eastern edge of the Ssu-shui's floodplain, where they rallied along a line of low cliffs. Li Shih-min's men launched a series of charges which failed to break them, though a handful of courageous troopers cut their way right through them and emerged in the rear of the Hsia line, riding back with arrows sticking in their armour 'like the quills of a porcupine'. Among these was one of Li Shih-min's cousins, Li Tao-hsuan, who performed this feat twice before returning to his commander on foot, his horse having been shot from under him. But still the Hsia stood their ground and reformed behind the returning cavalry, so Li Shih-min decided on another bold plan. He had nowhere near enough men to encircle the enemy, and small localised breakthroughs were not enough to break their cohesion, but perhaps he could make them believe that they were encircled. He gave Tao-hsuan another horse and ordered him to repeat his ride a third time, but on this occasion he followed in person with his bodyguard and all the banners of the T'ang army. When the little party emerged in the rear of the Hsia, they deliberately made as conspicuous a show as possible, waving their banners and shouting. Imagining that they were being surrounded and their retreat cut off, a few nearby Hsia units panicked and ran, and as the rumour spread, the rout gradually engulfed the whole line. Three thousand men were cut down as they tried to escape up the cliffs, while many more simply threw down their weapons and surrendered. Tou Chien-te's horse threw him in the confusion, and he was taken prisoner. Those who managed to climb the cliffs fled across the plain, but the T'ang horsemen pursued them for ten miles and killed many more. The Hsia army had been defeated by a far smaller but better led force, relying on boldness and bluff. It is likely that most of them never realised how few their opponents were. In contrast to his timid and indecisive opponent, Li Shih-min had not just commanded his army from a distance but had been in the thick of the fighting: a famous carved relief on his tomb shows his chestnut horse Shih-fa-ch'ih with five arrows sticking in his body, commemorating the fact that he had been wounded five times while carrying his master at the Battle of Ssu-shui.

The Victory of the T'ang

Over the next three years the T'ang consolidated its power throughout North China. The Hsia territory, and most of its surviving soldiers, were incorporated into the expanding empire. Tou Chien-te was taken back to Lo-yang and shown to his allies as a prisoner, whereupon Wang Shih-chung surrendered the city. Both men were subsequently executed. Li Shih-min's reward was to be appointed commander of the newly conquered lower Yellow River valley, with his headquarters at Lo-yang. From there he continued to campaign against the remaining independent warlords in the south, and by the end of 624 the empire was finally reunited under the rule of his father. But Li Yuan had made a fatal mistake by allowing his sons to establish themselves in the provinces at the head of their own private armies. Li Shih-min and his brothers, Chien-ch'eng and Yuan-chi, began to plot against each other, and their father seemed unable to control them. Matters came to a head early in 626, when a Turkish army invaded from the north-west and contingents were summoned to Ch'ang-an from the territories of all three princes to help defend the capital. Chien-ch'eng and Yuan-chi allegedly tried to bribe some of Shih-min's officers to assassinate him when he arrived in Ch'ang-an, but Shih-min learned of the plot and denounced both brothers to his father. When the emperor summoned them to answer the charges, they were killed in an ambush led by Shih-min, who is said to have personally shot Chien-ch'eng dead with his bow. Shih-min's troops occupied the city in the confusion, and Li Yuan was forced to abdicate in favour of his son, who took the throne as the Emperor T'ang T'ai-tsung. He reigned until his death in 649, and despite the dubious methods which he had used to obtain the throne, he has always been regarded as one of China's greatest emperors. In 627 the Turkish empire suddenly disintegrated owing to internal strife, and the T'ang seized the opportunity to extend their power deep into Central Asia. Another attack on Korea in 645 was less successful, but by the time of Li Shih-min's death the empire was wider in extent, more prosperous and more powerful than it had been since the great days of the Han.

Chapter Eight

China Confronts the West: Kao Hsien-Chih and the Battle of Atlakh, AD 751

Have you not seen, sir, out by the Koko Nor,
The white bones from ancient times that no one has gathered up?
The new ghosts bitterly complaining,
The old ghosts weep. Tu Fu.

The Chinese expansion into Central Asia which had begun under T'ang T'ai-tsung did not cease with his death. In fact it was during the reign of his successor Li Chi, who ruled as the Emperor Kao-tsung, that the T'ang Empire reached its greatest extent. In 651 the Western Turks, who had been temporarily subdued after the Battle of Bodgo-ola in 640, rebelled and invaded the Tarim Basin. Six years later a T'ang expeditionary force defeated them again at Lake Issyk-Kul in the T'ien Shan Mountains, and their Khagan was captured. The entire territory of the Western Turks was then organised into Chinese protectorates, which in theory took the frontier as far south and west as Herat in Afghanistan, and north to the shores of Lake Balkhash, in what is now Kazakhstan. In fact T'ang control in most of this area was never much more than nominal, and by 665 the Turks had recovered their de facto independence, but this move into the far west had inspired a continuing interest in controlling the eastern half of the Silk Road, and brought China into contact with several of the major powers of the region. Among these was Tibet, which had been organised into a centralised state by its king Gnam-ri-slon-mtshan and his son Sron-btsan-sgampo around the same time as the T'ang dynasty was consolidating its own power.

The Tibetan Campaigns

Although the Chinese records inevitably class them among the 'barbarians' of the steppes, the Tibetans thought of their own state as the equal of China, and in many ways they were justified in doing so. They were not yet much influenced by Buddhism, which was a later import from India, but they had their own system of writing, fortified cities, and extensive agriculture. They were famous as metal workers, which enabled them to equip large armies to a high standard. The T'ang Official History describes the Tibetan soldiers in these words: 'The men and horses all wear armour of excellent manufacture. It envelopes them completely, leaving only openings for the eyes. Thus strong bows and sharp swords cannot harm them.' Although they obviously thought it worthwhile to protect their horses, the Tibetans are described as normally dismounting to fight in ordered ranks, using swords, and lances which were longer and thinner than those of the Chinese. They also carried bows, but the T'ang history describes their archery as 'weak'. However Tibetan troops were exceptionally stubborn and unwilling to retreat, those in the rear instead stepping forward to take the place of any comrade who was killed.

During the seventh and eighth centuries Tibet established an extensive empire of its own, campaigning against – and often defeating – the Turks, and the city states of the Tarim Basin and the Pamirs. Its relationship with China was uneasy, sometimes being strengthened by treaties and marriage alliances, and sometimes degenerating into mutual raiding. Several pitched battles occurred, with both empires being victorious on different occasions. It was certainly not the case, as modern Chinese accounts have often claimed, that Tibet was ever a vassal of the T'ang. But in 736, concerned at Tibetan encroachments on the frontier which had been established by a peace treaty six years earlier, the T'ang Emperor Hsuan-tsung launched a major campaign with the aim of forcing the Tibetans to acknowledge his supremacy in Central Asia. At first the offensive was successful, but it soon bogged down in a series of bloody sieges, and the Chinese garrisons established in the west, around the Koko Nor Lake, found themselves blockaded by Tibetan cavalry, who waited until the grain sown by the invaders was ripe, then rode in to harvest it and leave the T'ang troops starving. It is likely that altitude sickness, the effects of which were mentioned in Chapter 5, also reduced the fighting effectiveness of Chinese troops operating on the Tibetan Plateau. So in 747 a new commander was appointed as 'Assistant Protector-General of the Pacified West', and despatched to restore the momentum. He was a Korean named Ko Sonji, known to the Chinese as Kao Hsien-chih, and he was to prove one of the most outstanding generals of the age.

Kao's objective was to outflank the Tibetans by occupying the minor kingdoms of Wakhan and Little Balur, situated in what is now northern Pakistan. Leading a force of only 10,000 men, consisting of both cavalry and infantry mounted on horses, he left Kucha in the Tarim Basin and marched south-west along the main ridge of the Pamir Mountains, one of the highest and most hostile ranges on earth. The journey took more than ninety-five days. Three days march away from the Tibetan fort at Lien-yun in Wakhan, in order to ease his supply difficulties, he divided his army into three detachments and ordered them to meet outside the fort on a specified day. This sort of co-ordination between separate columns was very difficult to achieve in the absence of modern communications, but everyone arrived on time, despite having to negotiate several flooded rivers en route. The fort was taken after a battle in which 5,000 Tibetans are said to have been killed. Kao then marched southwards to occupy Little Balur, but while on the march he received information that a larger Tibetan army was approaching from the east. Realising that the enemy would have to cross a deep gorge spanned by a bamboo suspension bridge, Kao raced to the western end of the bridge and ordered the cables to be cut. Unable to cross, the frustrated Tibetans retired. So far Kao's campaign had been a brilliant success. Not only had his march by a difficult mountain route taken the enemy completely by surprise, but on his arrival at his objective he had decisively outmanoeuvred greatly superior forces. Late in 749 he again defeated a Tibetan army and installed a pro-Chinese king on the throne of Chieh-shih, another little kingdom which had been threatening his communications with China. When the news reached Ch'ang-an the emperor awarded Kao the fitting title of 'Lord of the Mountains of China'. But it was his very success that encouraged Hsuan-tsung to involve Kao's tiny expedition in the far more dangerous waters of great power politics.

Tashkent and the Arabs

On the north-western side of the Pamir range two of the city states along the Silk Road, Ferghana and Tashkent, were engaged in a longstanding feud. The powerful Turgesh tribe, nomads of Turkish descent who were nominally vassals of the T'ang, sided with Tashkent, so the 'Ikhsid' or king of Ferghana appealed to Ch'ang-an for help. Some time in 750 the emperor sent a column of reinforcements to Kao Hsien-chih, bringing with them orders to cross the mountains and intervene in support of Ferghana. The Arab writer Ibn al-Athir, who incorrectly describes Kao as the 'king of China', says that he had 100,000 men with him, but it is unlikely that he had received anything like this number of reinforcements, or could have taken them across the inhospitable mountain passes if they had been available. The T'ang sources refer to 30,000 troops, both Chinese and foreign auxiliaries, many of whom were probably recruited on arrival in Ferghana. In any case a combined Chinese and Ferghanan army besieged Tashkent, and despite receiving its submission, Kao allowed his men to plunder the city and enslave its inhabitants. At the beginning of 751 he withdrew to the Tarim Basin and despatched the news of his victory to the emperor, along with a collection of illustrious captives. These included the Khagan of the Turgesh, the former kings of Tashkent and Chieh-shih, and several high-ranking Tibetan officers whose presence suggested that their emperor was also taking an interest in this 'proxy war' beyond the Pamirs. But the heir to the throne of Tashkent, a prince known to the Chinese as Yuan-en, was not among the prisoners. He had escaped from the city and fled to Samarkand, 200 miles to the south-west, where he begged the governor of the city for help.

Kao Hsien-chih had unwittingly come into conflict with the only power in Eurasia capable of meeting the T'ang on equal terms, for Ziyad ibn Salih al-Khuzai, the commander of the garrison in Samarkand, was an Arab. The rise of the Muslim Arabs inspired by the Prophet Muhammad was roughly contemporary with that of the T'ang and the Tibetans, but had been even more spectacular. Since the 620s the Muslims had conquered not only Arabia and most of the Byzantine Empire, but North Africa, Spain, and the vast territories once governed by the Sassanid dynasty of Persia. Samarkand had been captured by Qutayba ibn Muslim in 712, and three years later an Arab puppet king loyal to the Umayyad Caliphate in Damascus had been placed on the throne of Ferghana. However in the chaos following Qutayba's death at the hands of his mutinous soldiers, a Chinese-led expedition had driven out the Arab nominee and restored the previous ruler to power. In 737 the local pagan Turks had been decisively defeated by the Muslims, who then opened formal relations with China, with the result that the T'ang tacitly agreed to leave the region west of the Pamirs as an Arab sphere of influence. Then ten years later a rebellion broke out in the eastern territories of the Muslim Empire which led to the replacement of the Umayyad dynasty by the Abbasids, whose power base was in Iraq. For several years afterwards the Arabs were distracted by civil war, and in 750 Samarkand and the surrounding province of Khurasan had only recently been brought under Abbasid control. Now, however, the new dynasty was eager to re-establish its authority in the region. Ziyad listened to Yuan-en's pleas and immediately raised an army, sending a request to the governor of Khurasan, Abu Muslim, for reinforcements. In May 751 Abu Muslim's troops arrived in Samarkand, apparently giving rise to a report which reached Kao Hsien-chih soon afterwards, that the Arabs were massing an army to invade Chinese territory. So Kao marched back over the Pamirs in the hope of pre-empting this imaginary offensive, collecting allies on the way from among the Ferghanans and the Qarluq Turks.

The Abbasid Army

The core of the army which had brought the Abbasids to power was the heavy cavalry of the 'ahl Khurasan', recruited from the province of that name. Despite their title these were not drawn from the native Iranian and Turkish people of Khurasan, but from Arab settlers, many of them second or third generation descendants of the original armies of conquest. Arab cavalry traditionally wore mail armour and fought at close quarters with swords and lances, though they seem to have done so in loose formations, advancing and retiring when necessary in an attempt to wear down the enemy, rather than charging en masse. If outnumbered they would dismount to ward off enemy horsemen with a phalanx of grounded spears. By the 750s they had begun to adopt the styles of armour and equipment of the native Khurasanis, who were equipped in Turkish style with lances, composite bows, and often metal armour for both man and horse. However it appears that if the Arabs did try to adopt their mounted archery tactics they enjoyed little success, because al-Jahiz, writing a few decades later, describes them as having 'no skill worth mentioning in shooting from horseback'. He goes on to say that a thousand local Khurasani horse-archers could easily shoot down a similar number of Arabs without loss, but it has been deduced from artistic representations that even the Khurasanis preferred to charge with their lances rather than shoot from a distance. Similarly equipped Persian horsemen, probably refugees from the Sassanid Empire which had been conquered by the Arabs in the 630s, had fought against the invaders of Khurasan in the late seventh century, and their descendants may still have been serving with some of the city states. The Arab infantry, which had declined in importance since the Umayyad period but still outnumbered the horsemen by about two to one, was armed with spears and bows, and could be mounted on horses, mules or camels for strategic mobility. Tactically it provided a solid defensive base from which the men who fought on horseback could operate. This system was remarkably similar to that of the T'ang Chinese, described in Chapter 7, and it may be partly for that reason that the battle which they were about to fight was so indecisive for so long.

The Battle of Atlakh

The ensuing confrontation between the Arabs and the Chinese has usually been referred to in western accounts as the Battle of Talas, after the city and river of that name, but it seems to have involved extensive manoeuvring over a wide expanse of territory over the course of several days, which tends to support the idea that most if not all of the combatants were mounted (Beckwith). In the last week of July 751, Kao Hsien-chih's forces clashed with an Arab advance guard under the command of Sa'd ibn Hamid, not far from the city of Talas. Sa'd appears to have stood on the defensive, until the approach of the main army led by Ziyad ibn Salih forced the Chinese to fall back on their own supports. Kao then deployed for battle around the town of Atlakh, and the next day Ziyad attacked him there. T'ang sources say that the fighting lasted for five days, with no significant advantage gained by either side. This certainly suggests skirmishing tactics, whether or not the Arabs and their allies were exchanging missiles with Kao's troops from a distance or attempting to deliver blows with swords or lances. Neither army seems to have fielded an equivalent of the fully armoured charging cavalry that had dominated the warfare of sixth century China, and which might have forced a decision much sooner. The experience of European medieval, eighteenth century and Napoleonic warfare shows that heavy cavalry, with their vital parts protected by armour, often suffered very light casualties in combat against their equivalents, and two sides so equipped skirmishing at a distance could easily do so for a protracted period without either being seriously weakened.

Finally, on the fifth day of fighting, the stalemate was broken when the Qarluq Turks suddenly defected en masse to the Arabs. The Chinese, now outnumbered, succeeded in extricating themselves under cover of darkness and fell back to their camp, where Kao held a hurried council of war. He was apparently proposing to resume the fight on the following day despite the odds against him, but his deputy commander, Li Ssu-yeh, persuaded him that this course would inevitably lead to the annihilation of his army. The next morning, therefore, the T'ang began a retreat to the east along a narrow track leading across a range of hills which the Chinese called the Pai-shih Ling, or White Stone Mountains. But the Ferghanans had got there first, blocking the pass with their baggage animals and retreating troops. Li Ssu-yeh, at the head of the Chinese cavalry, literally cut his way through, hacking and beating their former allies to death until the survivors abandoned the path and allowed them through. Thanks to this ruthless act Kao Hsien-chih and many of his senior officers escaped, but several thousand of the Chinese rank-and-file were overtaken by the victorious Muslims and captured.

The Chinese prisoners seem on the whole to have been well treated, and as is well known, some of those incarcerated in Samarkand taught the Arabs the secret of making paper – a transfer of technology to the west that would eventually have momentous consequences. Another prisoner of war, Tu Huan, travelled as far as Baghdad, and after his release in 762 returned to Ch'ang-an and wrote a book about his experiences.

Kao Hsien-chih salvaged his reputation from the defeat, and continued to command Chinese armies in the civil war which was to follow. But the T'ang never returned west of the Pamirs. The only recorded battle of pre-modern times between a great Chinese dynasty and its western equivalent had ended in a disastrous Chinese defeat.

Chapter Nine

Shaking the Empire: Ch'ang-An and Lo-Yang, AD 756 to 757

'One who takes pleasure in war will perish, and one who covets the spoils of victory will incur disgrace. War is not something to be enjoyed, and victory is not something to profit from.' Sun Pin.

T'ang Decline

By the middle of the eighth century, the 'fu-ping' militia system which had served the early T'ang emperors so well had suffered a significant decline in efficiency and importance. To a great extent this was a consequence of the defensive posture which the empire had now been forced to adopt. The aggressive campaigns of Li Shih-min and his immediate successors had taken China up to its natural frontiers – and in some places well beyond them – while at the same time stimulating the rise of powerful rivals like the Tibetans. The result was that T'ang forces were now more likely to be deployed permanently in the border regions as defensive garrisons, rather than being recruited for short offensive campaigns. In these circumstances part-time soldiers who were called up for specific terms were clearly an unsatisfactory source of manpower, especially as most of the 'fu-ping' were based in the main Chinese population centres along the lower Yellow River, and had to march great distances to reach their posts on the frontiers. It was also difficult to muster them quickly in response to an invasion threat, and supplying large armies stationed in the arid regions of Central Asia presented an equally intractable problem. Therefore, as early as the end of the seventh century, commanders of the remoter garrisons began to recruit full-time professional troops known as 'chien-erh', or 'strong men', to supplement the militia. These men were volunteers drawn from the whole Chinese population, although they included many re-enlisted militiamen. The system was regularised in 710, when the frontier districts were organised into nine regional commands, each under a governor having responsibility for both the garrisons and a mobile defence army. Most of the manpower was now supplied by long-service 'chien-erh' troops, and the supply difficulties were eased by the traditional expedient of employing the men in growing crops when they were not on campaign. By 737 the border armies were supposed to consist entirely of professionals, and the 'fu-ping' was formally abolished in 749, although there is evidence that local militias were still sometimes called up in times of crisis. Also increasingly important were foreign auxiliaries, and we have already seen how Ferghanan and Turkish cavalry played a vital role in many of the Central Asian campaigns.

Attempts were also made to put the officer class on a more professional footing, and as early as 702 examinations were introduced for officer candidates. However the emphasis was mainly on physical strength and individual skill with the bow and lance, and although there was an oral examination in leadership skills, it seems that the ability to set a personal example in combat was considered far more important. This is borne out by accounts in the T'ang histories of the lives of several high-ranking commanders. Chang Wan-fu, for example, came from a family of scholars, but none of them had been particularly successful in their careers. So Chang abandoned his books, and instead studied horsemanship and archery. He volunteered for the army, and after distinguishing himself in a single campaign was promoted to the rank of general.

From the narrow point of view of military strategy, these reforms were fairly successful. However their very success was to undermine the T'ang regime from within. The 'fu-ping' militia system had helped to strengthen the central government, providing as it did a source of manpower close to the capital and mustered at the command of the emperor. Now the strongest and most experienced troops were on the frontiers, permanently under the control of semi-independent governors. Originally the military governors were overseen by civilian officials whose job was to ensure their loyalty, but gradually the governors began to use their influence to sideline these overseers, or even to take over their positions and in effect to oversee themselves. Naturally the T'ang emperor Hsuan-tsung, who inherited this system when he came to the throne in 712, was well aware of the risk that these men might rebel, and either establish their own states or attempt to take over the entire empire. One of his proposed solutions, however, was eventually to turn this very real risk into a certainty.

Talented officers of non-Chinese origin had been employed in the T'ang armies since the early days of the dynasty, but by the middle of the eighth century they were increasingly to be found at the highest levels of the command structure. One reason for this was the belief that they were aloof from Chinese power politics, and so more likely to be loyal to the dynasty. A successful example of this policy was of course the Korean general Kao Hsien-chih, whose campaigns in Central Asia have been discussed in Chapter 8. Another eminent foreign general was An Lu-shan, who rose to command local forces on the north-eastern frontier in the early 740s. An was a Sogdian, originally from Bokhara in Central Asia, but his mother was Turkish, and he had been brought up in China by an uncle. By 733 he was an officer in the frontier army, where he gained a reputation for recklessness, but this clearly did not hinder his advancement. In 744, newly appointed as governor of Fanyang, he travelled to Ch'ang-an where he attracted the attention of Hsuan-tsung's chief minister, Li Lin-fu. Li was by now the most powerful personality in the empire as the ageing Hsuan-tsung increasingly withdrew from public affairs. He had many enemies among the Chinese generals, and apparently believed that An Lu-shan would be a useful ally. He therefore arranged for his rapid promotion, and by 751 An had been awarded the title of Prince, and been placed in command of all the north-eastern frontier armies. Then in 752 Li Lin-fu died and was succeeded by Yang Kuo-chung, the cousin of the emperor's favourite concubine Yang Kuei-fei. The new chief minister seems to have been unhappy about the power which was now concentrated in the hands of An Lu-shan, although it is not clear whether he was actively plotting to remove him, or whether An merely suspected him of doing so. Either way, the Sogdian warlord now felt out of his depth and vulnerable in the world of court intrigue. There was particular hostility between him and the commander on the Tibetan frontier, Qosu Khan, despite the fact that the latter was also of mixed Sogdian and Turkish descent. The T'ang Official History tells of An's unsuccessful attempt at arranging a reconciliation with Qosu by reminding him of this shared heritage in the presence of the emperor. But in December 755, fearing for his position if not for his life, An mustered his army and announced to his officers that he had been ordered by the emperor to remove the 'treacherous bandit', Yang Kuo-chung.

An Lu-shan's Rebellion

Hsuan-tsung had issued no such order, and the rising threw the court into panic. Generals were despatched to the interior provinces to raise new troops, and the frontier armies of the north-west were summoned to march to the defence of Ch'ang-an. The emperor also took his revenge on An's family who were living in the capital, having his son executed and driving his wife to suicide. An commanded an estimated 150,000 troops, many of them battle-hardened veterans, including a bodyguard of 8,000 'barbarian' (probably Turkish) horsemen. Leaving around a third of his strength to guard the frontier, he led the rest south on a rapid march to strike the Yellow River at Pien-chou, south of Lo-yang. This town controlled the junction of the river with the northern end of the Grand Canal built by the Sui emperors 150 years earlier, and through it passed vital supplies of food from the south to the northern cities of Lo-yang and Ch'ang-an. Not only were these supplies now cut off, but it was here that An learned of the fate of his family. In his fury he slaughtered the entire garrison of Pien-chou, then marched upriver towards Lo-yang.

Facing him there was the T'ang general Feng Ch'ang-ch'ing, who had raised an army of 60,000 local levies to defend the city. Feng was an able commander but his troops were inexperienced, and in several battles along the river they failed to stand against An Lu-shan's veterans. In July 756 the rebels reached Lo-yang and captured it. Feng fell back westwards to the famous defensive position at the T'ong Pass, which he found already occupied by a loyalist army under the command of Kao Hsien-chih. This position was too strong for the rebels to attack, so they retreated a few miles to the east and set up a fortified camp of their own on the plain. Nevertheless An now felt secure enough to reveal his true plans, and proclaimed himself the founder of the 'Greater Yen' dynasty, adopting the name of the state which had controlled the far north-eastern districts of China in the Warring States era. He attempted to establish a formal system of government in the province of Honan, south of the Yellow River, though further north, where his armies had passed through too quickly to consolidate their conquests, some 200,000 pro-T'ang troops remained in the field. An sent an army back to subdue them under his trusted deputy Shi Ssu-ming, but it was defeated, and the loyalists continued to launch harassing attacks on his lines of communication. The rebels' offensive had stalled, and the T'ang were gradually recovering the initiative. It was to take a series of foolish miscalculations by the emperor and his chief minister to restore the impetus of the revolt.

Hsuan-tsung had successfully ruled China for more than forty years, earning from his subjects the title of the 'Brilliant Emperor', but his behaviour in this crisis suggests that he was no longer entirely sane. Kao Hsien-chih and Feng Ch'ang-ch'ing had wisely remained on the defensive in their impregnable position in the T'ong Pass, but the emperor chose to regard their passive stance as treachery. He had them both arrested and executed, placing An Lu-shan's old enemy Qosu Khan in command in their place. At first Qosu also refused to abandon the defensive strategy, but eventually the emperor ordered him to attack,

on pain of death. Apparently the idea came from Yang Kuo-chung, who was afraid that like An Lu-shan, Qosu was planning to replace the T'ang with his own 'barbarian' dynasty, and took this opportunity to weaken his forces. If so, it was a remarkably short-sighted decision. Qosu now had 180,000 men, including his own crack troops from the Tibetan frontier army, but it is likely that most of his units were composed of inexperienced and demoralised levies. He advanced into the plain, but

The technique for cocking and loading the crossbow, illustrated on a Han dynasty stamped tile excavated at Chengchou in Honan. Such reliefs were often placed in tombs, perhaps as a warning to illiterate robbers that the treasures within were booby-trapped. Note the bolt held in the figure's teeth while he stands on the bow and pulls up on the string with both hands.

was ambushed and eventually surrounded by the rebels. Qosu's army was destroyed, and he was captured and later executed by his old rival. Hsuan-tsung had now managed to dispose of his three most talented generals. The defeat left the pass unguarded, and An's army poured through almost unopposed.

As the rebels approached Ch'ang-an the emperor panicked. He, Chief Minister Yang Kuo-chung and the concubine Yang Kuei-fei fled with a bodyguard of loyal soldiers, aiming for Szechwan in the far south-west of China. When their departure was discovered the remaining garrison in the capital mutinied and began to loot the city, and in the confusion An Lu-shan's men broke in and massacred the inhabitants. Meanwhile at Ma-wei the fleeing emperor met a friendly Tibetan embassy on its way to Ch'ang-an. It might be thought that Hsuan-tsung would welcome any friends he could find, but – whether on his orders or not is not clear – his bodyguard instead slaughtered all the Tibetans. They then turned on Yang Kuo-chung, accusing him of being in league with the foreigners, and killed him also. Finally they demanded the execution of Yang Kuei-fei, to which the emperor reluctantly agreed. Then the party split up, the demoralised Hsuan-tsung continuing south to Szechwan while his heir, the Crown Prince Li Heng, rode west to the outpost of Ling-wu on the Tibetan border with the aim of continuing the fight. On arrival at Ling-wu, however, Li Heng proclaimed himself emperor under the name Su-tsung. When this news reached Hsuan-tsung he meekly agreed to abdicate, bringing a reign of almost half a century to an inglorious end. The Tibetans, already antagonised by the former emperor's aggressive policy in Central Asia, and now encouraged by the removal of Qosu Khan's army, quickly moved to capture the forts which Qosu had built along the border, and advanced eastwards along the upper reaches of the Yellow River as far as Hsi-p'ing, within striking distance of Ch'ang-an. This move effectively cut China off from Central Asia and the trade routes to the west. For the moment, however, the Tibetan armies did not take further advantage of the chaos in China, and even sent a small contingent to help the T'ang forces fighting to suppress the rebels.

The T'ang Fight Back

Meanwhile, in a series of actions on the fringes of An Lu-shan's 'Greater Yen Empire', forces loyal to the T'ang began to contain the rebels and fight back. Two stories told of one of these loyalist commanders, Chang Hsun, illustrate the imaginative approach to warfare which the Chinese have always admired. Early in 756 Chang Hsun had retaken the city of Yung-ch'iu on the southern fringe of An Lu-shan's new domain, only to be besieged there when the rebel general Ch'ao Ling-hu returned with an army of 40,000 men. Ch'ao deployed siege engines which hurled missiles against the city walls and breached them, but Chang built wooden palisades to replace them, and by launching sorties against the enemy forced them to give up the siege temporarily and retire. Shortly afterwards Ch'ao returned with reinforcements, but the outnumbered defenders still held out. Then, after forty days of fighting, Chang Hsun realised that they were running out of arrows. These were not easy items to improvise, since a bow is useless without arrows of the correct length and stiffness, and not all wood is strong or flexible enough for the purpose. It was common practice to reuse and return the enemy's arrows during a prolonged archery duel, but troops inside a fortification were always at a disadvantage in such an exchange, since fewer enemy missiles landed inside the defences where they could reach them. Of course the besiegers were also more likely to have access to the raw materials with which to make more arrows. So Chang ordered his men to make 1,000 straw dummies, and when darkness fell to let them down over the city walls on ropes. Supposing that the T'ang soldiers were trying to escape, the rebel archers eagerly took up their bows and riddled these easy targets with arrows. Then the defenders pulled the straw men back up the wall with their haul of free ammunition. It is perhaps unlikely that this clever stratagem provided enough arrows to solve the problem for long, but by making the rebels look foolish it must at least have boosted the defenders' morale. Later the same night another 500 figures were seen descending the walls on ropes. The rebel sentries were not going to be fooled a second time, and decided not to raise the alarm. But on this occasion the 500 were real soldiers, picked from the bravest men in Chang's army. When they reached the ground they drew their swords and charged into the rebel camp, killing many of the enemy before they could grab their weapons, and spreading terror among the survivors. After this setback Ch'ao Ling-hu again raised the siege, abandoning any hope of spreading the rebellion further south.

In the following year Chang Hsun once again found himself besieged, this time at Sui-yang. After being blockaded for twenty days by a rebel army led by Yin Chi-ch'i, he led a surprise night attack with his cavalry, allegedly killing 5,000 of the enemy rank and file and fifty officers. This sortie demoralised the rebels but Yin persisted with the siege, so Chang decided to eliminate him personally. However he was not able to identify his target by sight; presumably Yin was aware of the risk of assassination, and either employed decoys or dressed in a way that was indistinguishable from his officers. So Chang decided to run out of arrows again. He had his men shoot a volley of crude wooden sticks into the besiegers' lines, in order to give the impression that they were out of proper ammunition. Several of the rebels could be seen picking up these sticks and running to report the good news to their commander. As soon as he was identified, one of Chang's best archers targeted Yin with a real arrow. The rebel general was hit in the eye and killed, and his men abandoned the siege.

Other T'ang strongholds also succeeded in holding out and frustrating the rebels' attempts to overrun the rest of the empire. Notable among these was Sung-chou on the Huai River, which blocked the route into the fertile lands along the lower Yangtze. The new Emperor Su-tsung mounted two attempts to retake Ch'ang-an during the winter of 756 to 757, but failed on both occasions and suffered heavy losses. However An Lu-shan's advance had now lost its momentum, and the rebels turned increasingly to fighting among themselves. An himself was murdered by his own troops in January 757, and although his son An Ch'ing-hsu succeeded him as 'emperor', he lacked his father's commanding presence and seems never to have re-established central control over the various widely scattered rebel armies. The T'ang were also fighting on several separate fronts, and in the summer of 757 the war seemed to be degenerating into a series of independent campaigns between local warlords on both sides. In one of these the Prince of Lin, a younger son of Hsuan-tsung who commanded a fleet of ships on the Yangtze River, tried to use them in an unsuccessful coup against the emperor.

But Emperor Su-tsung was taking advantage of the stalemate to amass a new army for another attempt on Ch'ang-an. He had also been busy establishing diplomatic relations with neighbouring powers, as a result of which he received substantial reinforcements from outside the empire, including Uighurs from Central Asia, Khotanese from the Tarim Basin, and even Arabs sent by the Abbasid Caliph in Baghdad. The most useful of these contingents consisted of 4,000 Uighur cavalry, led by their crown prince or 'Yabgu'. The Uighurs were a Turkish people from what is now Mongolia, who had achieved independence in 744 when a revolt by various disaffected tribes destroyed the Khanate of the Eastern Turks. Many of the Uighurs were townsmen and farmers rather than nomads, and they went on to develop a settled civilisation of their own, including their own system of writing. Later, in the Mongol period, they apparently served mainly as infantry, but the men who fought for the T'ang were typically Turkish mounted archers, the richer warriors at least wearing armour, and backing up their bows with swords, shields and lances. The An Lu-shan rebellion, and the simultaneous Tibetan incursions into the Ordos region, had cut off the T'ang armies from most of their best horse-breeding areas, and their mounted arm would never again equal the heavy cavalry of the seventh century in either numbers or skill. Therefore the relatively small band of Uighurs became the principal striking force of Su-tsung's army, and was to a large extent responsible for his subsequent victories. Remarkably, the Uighurs were able to provide support for the T'ang while being at the same time engaged in a desperate war on their northern frontier against the Kirghiz, whose 50,000 strong army they decisively defeated in 758.

The Battles of Hsiang-chi and Hsin-tien, 757

The first of these victories took place in November 757, at Hsiang-chi on the banks of the Feng River. The T'ang army was commanded by the Prince of Kuang-p'ing and General Kuo Tzu-i. Both armies established their camps on the open plain and deployed for a pitched battle, but the rebels had hidden a unit of picked cavalry on their right or eastern flank, with the aim of attacking the T'ang left from the rear once the battle was joined. However the T'ang left wing commander spotted them and brought up the Uighurs, who instead took the ambushers in the rear and annihilated them. Then, reinforced by Chinese units, they outflanked the rebel right. The rebels' own tactic was now employed against them, and their army, attacked from two directions at once, was defeated. Ch'ang-an was left undefended, and on the following day it was retaken by imperial forces.

The Yabgu's men were not allowed to enter the capital, as the Prince of Kuang-p'ing feared that they would plunder it. Instead he sent the Uighurs eastwards on an outflanking move against Lo-yang. At Ch'u-wo they discovered another force of rebels hidden in ambush in a valley on the side of a mountain, took them by surprise and rode them down. Meanwhile General Kuo Tzu-i, advancing along a parallel route, had encountered an enormous enemy army at Hsin-tien and had been forced to retreat, but the Uighurs crossed over the mountain and appeared unexpectedly in the rebel rear, their white banners flying. Once again the enemy were caught between two forces, and it is unlikely that in the confusion they ever realised how few the Uighurs were. They broke and fled northwards, pursued for miles by the triumphant T'ang troops. It was said that men and horses trampled each other in the rout, and that no fewer than 100,000 corpses were scattered across the countryside for a distance of thirty 'li', or about ten miles. When they received the news of this catastrophic defeat the rebels abandoned Lo-yang, and this time the Uighurs were the first inside the gates. The Prince of Kuang-p'ing's fears proved fully justified, as the 'barbarians' systematically looted the city for three days before order was finally restored, carrying off an immense quantity of plunder.

The prince had counted on reprovisioning his exhausted army with supplies captured in Lo-yang, but the rebels had already destroyed many of them, and the remainder disappeared into the hands of the Uighurs. This was one of the factors which prevented him from following up his victories and invading the rebel stronghold in the north-east. Instead he took his men into winter quarters and offered an amnesty, which led to the surrender of An's deputy Shi Ssu-ming early in 758. The remaining rebels were concentrated in the city of Hsiang-chou, where T'ang forces besieged them in the autumn of that year, but the siege dragged on until the spring of 759, when Shi Ssu-ming, who had temporarily transferred his allegiance to the T'ang, changed sides again. He brought his army down from the north to raise the siege, and by attacking during a dust storm managed to surprise and rout the T'ang army. Shi then recaptured Lo-yang, executed An Ch'ing-hsu, and took over the leadership of the rebel armies himself. Again the war bogged down in stalemate, with the T'ang emperor based at Ch'ang-an and his rival at Lo-yang, neither being strong enough to threaten the other's capital. But now the T'ang could afford to wait, because the ramshackle regime established by An Lu-shan and his successors had held together only as long as its armies were advancing, giving the soldiers access to new supplies of loot. Now they began to desert, or accept the amnesties offered by the government, in ever larger numbers. Shi was killed in April 761 and replaced by his son, who remained in power until November 762, when he met a T'ang army in battle outside Lo-yang and was defeated, whereupon his leading generals all surrendered. After five years of fighting the empire was once again united, at least for the time being. But the miscalculations of the T'ang authorities, and the greed of their protégés, had cost China incalculable amounts of treasure, and perhaps millions of lives. The censuses taken in 754 and 766 recorded a reduction in the estimated population of the empire, based on the numbers of households, from more than fifty million to less than twenty million. Most of the losses were probably not direct casualties of war, but refugees, people left too impoverished to be worth taxing, or those unfortunates who had died of starvation or disease in the wake of the armies. Nevertheless the suffering and destruction were catastrophic, and the regime which had allowed the disaster to happen would never fully regain the confidence of its people.

The End of the T'ang

The rebellion of An Lu-shan was not the last of the upheavals that shook the T'ang empire to its foundations during the eighth century. In 763 a Tibetan army briefly seized Ch'ang-an, appointed a puppet emperor and drove off the horses from the imperial stud farms in the vicinity, further weakening the already declining Chinese cavalry arm. Then in a series of revolts in the 780s the T'ang almost lost control of the Yellow River plain altogether, and after that the process of decentralisation that had begun at the end of the previous century reached its culmination. The small and increasingly overstretched imperial armies were concentrated in the region of the vulnerable capital, leaving the task of frontier defence to local magnates of dubious loyalty. In the confusion a horde of Turks belonging to the Sha-t'o tribe settled in the north, where they were tolerated as a buffer against other invaders from the steppe, and as a source of desperately needed mounted mercenaries. For a while the residual prestige of the T'ang royal house prevented the complete disintegration of the empire, and during the early ninth century the imperial armies regained some lost ground in the provinces, but in 874 the rebellion of Huang Chao finally brought the system to the point of collapse. Huang Chao was defeated by the armies of two provincial commanders, Chu Wen and the Sha-t'o Turk Li K'o-yung, but once peace was restored these men did not disband their forces but instead employed them in a power struggle against each other, with the T'ang rulers as helpless spectators. Eventually, in 907, Chu Wen deposed the last T'ang emperor and proclaimed his own dynasty, which he named the Later Liang.

Chapter Ten

Siege at a Distance: The Huan-Erh-Tsui Campaign and the Fall of Chung-T'u, AD 1211 to 1215

'Nothing is more difficult than the art of manoeuvre. What is difficult about manoeuvre is to make the devious route the most direct and to turn misfortune to advantage.' Sun Tzu.

The Return of the Barbarians

The half century after the fall of the T'ang has become known to history as the 'Five Dynasties and Ten Kingdoms', a title which aptly conveys the extent of the political fragmentation of the time. The 'Five Dynasties', two of which were established by 'emperors' of Sha-t'o Turkish descent, succeeded each other in rapid succession in the north of the country, while the south was divided among ten independent, and generally mutually hostile, native Chinese states. Meanwhile the Khitans, a people from beyond the north-eastern frontier who in 907 were newly united under their own emperor Yeh-lu A-pao-chi, occupied several districts in north-east China and established their own Chinese-style regime, the Liao. In 960 Chao K'uang-yin reunified most of China under the Sung dynasty, but he was unable to dislodge the Khitans. In 1004 the latter invaded Sung territory, but were forced to withdraw after a bloody encounter at Shan-chou, and the two rival states made peace. By then, however, a more serious threat to the Sung had arisen in the north-west. There the Tanguts, a people of partly Tibetan origin, were also moving into what had once been the Chinese heartland, this time via the upper reaches of the Yellow River. Here they again took over the horse breeding areas of the Ordos, whose loss to the Tibetans had been so disastrous to the T'ang. Over the next century the Sung and the Tanguts – whose rulers styled themselves Emperors of Hsi-Hsia, or Western Hsia, thus claiming a connection with the legendary Hsia dynasty – fought a series of ferocious wars which merely succeeded in further weakening the Sung. After a disastrous defeat at Tsang-ti Ho in 1115 the Sung abandoned their attempts to reconquer the lands of Hsi-Hsia, but by then events on the north-eastern frontier had once again overtaken them.

The Jurchen and the Golden Dynasty

In 1114 a tribe known as the Jurchen, who had been forced to pay tribute to the Liao, revolted against their masters under the leadership of their chief, Wan-yen Akuta. The Jurchen were distant relatives of the Hsien-pi of old, whose homeland was in the forests of what is now Manchuria. There they grew crops and raised cattle, and although their Chinese neighbours typically disparaged them as 'barbarians', they seem to have absorbed a great deal of the political and military organisation of the more centralised states around them. Whatever the reason, they quickly proved a match for the Khitans. The Sung Emperor Hui-tsung seized the opportunity to attack the Khitans from the rear while they were preoccupied with the Jurchen threat, and the Liao regime collapsed under the two-pronged assault. However it was the Jurchen and not the Sung who took over the territory of the vanquished, and by 1125 the former 'barbarians' found themselves masters of the whole Liao Empire. In its place they set up their own Chinese-style dynasty, named the Chin, or 'Golden'. Hui-tsung's strategy had backfired disastrously, because in contrast to the Liao the Chin were aggressively expansionist, and their armies did not stop at the Sung frontier. In 1127 they captured the emperor and his capital, K'ai-feng, and drove the Sung forces in disarray south of the Yangtze River. The war continued until 1141, when the Sung signed a humiliating peace which left the invaders in control of the whole of North China, which they were to hold for the next seventy years. During that time the Chin became a true Chinese dynasty in a way that their Khitan predecessors had never done, as the Jurchen enthusiastically adopted the manners of the Sung elite, and Chinese officials were retained to administer their empire along traditional lines. K'ai-feng quickly recovered from the conquest and resumed its role as a great trading city, but the newcomers preferred to maintain some ties with their origins in the north, and so the main seat of government was transferred to Chung-tu, in what was then the remote north-east, on the site of the modern capital of Beijing. It was at Chung-tu, in the second decade of the thirteenth century, that China first confronted the last and greatest of the invasions from the steppes.

Chinggis Khan and the Mongols

By that time, paradoxically, the Chung-tu region had not been under native Chinese control for more than three centuries, and it was to the Jurchen that the task fell of holding the line against the new threat. In yet another paradox, it had been Jurchen interference in the affairs of the northern nomads that had brought this threat into being. Over the previous few centuries the Turkish peoples who had once dominated the Mongolian steppe had dispersed, either southwards, where they became integrated into Chinese civilisation, or west beyond the Pamirs, where they had adopted Islam and become embroiled in the power politics of the Middle East. On either side of the T'ien Shan Mountains stretched the Kara-Khitai Empire, a rather shaky conglomeration of Turks, Uighurs and refugee Khitans, but further east the grasslands north of what had once been the Chinese frontier was left to poor and politically fragmented bands of Tatars, Naimans, Keraits, Merkits, and other horse- and cattle-breeding nomads who became collectively known as Mongols. The Chin frontier ran much further north than that of most native Chinese dynasties, and they also maintained close links with their homeland in Manchuria. In order to secure these possessions they attempted to extend their hegemony into Mongolia by supporting the Tatars against their rivals. This policy, however, backfired when a talented leader named Temuchin, whose family had a bitter feud with the Tatars, succeeded in unifying the Mongol tribes in 1206. Temuchin then adopted the name by which he is better known, Chinggis (or Genghis) Khan, and publicly repudiated the allegiance which his people had theoretically owed to the Chin. *The Secret History of the Mongols*, our main source for these events from the Mongol side, relates that when he was informed of the accession of a new emperor, Wei-shao, instead of bowing as custom demanded, Chinggis spat in the direction of China and asked rhetorically why he should be expected to kowtow to such a weakling. The omens were not good for future relations, but for the next few years the newly united Mongols were fully occupied in campaigning against Hsi Hsia. There they learned valuable preliminary lessons in the art of attacking walled cities, but without siege engines they were unable to capture the capital Yin-ch'uan, and in 1209 Chinggis made a negotiated peace, according to which the Tanguts became his vassals and agreed to supply troops for his army. Then, in the spring of 1211, a Mongol army which Chinese sources estimated at 100,000 strong started south across the Gobi Desert on its way to attack the Chin.

The Mongol Army

On this occasion the Chinese may not have greatly exaggerated the numbers of their enemies, because Chinggis had succeeded in mobilising the resources of the steppe tribes as none of their leaders had ever done before. He and many of his leading subordinates had started their careers as fugitives with no tribal power base, but paradoxically this was to be one of the secrets of Chinggis' success: with no traditional political structure to worry about, he could start from scratch and organise his forces in a new way. They were grouped not by tribe but into units of tens, hundreds, thousands and ten thousands, and commanded by men promoted on the basis of merit rather than noble birth. This system was able to incorporate steppe nomads of non-Mongol origin with a minimum of trouble, enabling ever bigger forces to be raised as the conquests gathered pace. An account in *The Secret History* of the organisation of the army in 1206 suggests a total of about 105,000 for the contingents of the various Mongol tribes. Already by 1211 these were being supplemented by Turks, Tanguts and others, and soon disaffected Khitans, Uighurs and even Chinese were to join them. These large, coherent armies, rather than any particular Mongol ferocity, were the real key to Chinggis' success. In contrast to many of the earlier steppe hordes they were also highly disciplined, with a formal command hierarchy and a well developed system of communications. The armies were accompanied by large herds of remounts, which gave them exceptional strategic and tactical mobility. Messengers mounted on fast horses were employed to maintain contact between widely separated forces, an innovation which permitted complex strategic manoeuvres on an almost Napoleonic scale. Like their other institutions of government, the organisation of the Mongol army may have owed much to the example of the Uighurs, whose system of writing was also borrowed for the Mongol bureaucracy.

But, like their predecessors on the steppe, the Mongol soldiers continued to rely principally on mounted archery. They were renowned for their powerful bows. The rest of their equipment seems to have been fairly primitive at this stage, though they do seem to have been happy to fight hand-to-hand when necessary. In 1216 Shah Muhammad of the Muslim empire of Khwarizmia was victorious in an engagement with a small Mongol reconnaissance party, but was left unnerved by the ferocious resistance he had encountered, complaining that 'he had never seen men as daring nor as steadfast in the throes of battle, or as skilled in giving blows with the point and edge of the sword' (Martin). The Franciscan friar John de Plano Carpini, who travelled to Mongolia in the 1240s, describes lances with hooks below the head for hauling opponents out of their saddles, but these were obviously in short supply, as he goes on to say that most Mongols carried only a bow and a small axe. Body armour and helmets were known, but were probably mostly of leather, though the Sung writer Meng Hung claims that one reason for the Mongols' success was that they possessed more iron than previous steppe peoples. Much of this metal, in fact, had originally come from China. Earlier dynasties had imposed an embargo on selling iron to the 'barbarians', but the Jurchen had ceased to enforce this. At the same time the Chin rulers had refused to recognise the iron money minted by their Sung rivals as legal tender, so their Chinese subjects had disposed of their holdings of this currency as scrap, to merchants who sold it on to the Mongols. It seems that Chinese money, reforged into weapons and armour, had helped to equip the armies which were now invading China.

The Forces of Jurchen China

Before the conquest of the Liao the Jurchen had fought exclusively on horseback, organised into tribal units known as 'Meng-an mou-k'o', or 'units of a thousand and a hundred'. When they later took over extensive settled districts these units became the basis of military-agricultural colonies, with a group of families allocated to provide recruits and supplies for each fighting unit. A 'meng-an' of a thousand men was made up of ten 'mou-k'o', each of which was divided into two fifty-man 'p'u-nien'. The traditional fighting formation of the Jurchen cavalry was based on the 'p'u-nien' and was known as the 'kuai-tzu ma', or 'horse team'. This was a five-rank deep formation, with armoured lancers in the first two ranks, probably wearing long lamellar coats of the type that had been in use in China since the T'ang, and more lightly protected mounted archers behind. (This formation has sometimes been ascribed to the Mongols as well, but with little or no supporting evidence (Martin).) An unlikely story that the Jurchen horsemen fought chained together, like the Mu-jung of the fourth century, was probably derived from a misunderstanding of their habit of manoeuvring in dense formations, maintaining close co-operation between different units. The Jurchen usually deployed in three large bodies, a centre and two wings, and it is likely that their normal practice was to drive off horse-archer armies with a charge to close quarters, sometimes led by the commander in person. At the Battle of Lung Shan in 1215, for example, the Chin general Ta Lu led a charge against his Mongol counterpart, and succeeded in unhorsing him before being killed.

As often happened with alien regimes in China, the cavalry declined over the years as the tribal nobility became landed gentry and settled in areas more suitable for agriculture than horse breeding. For this reason the entirely mounted armies of the conquest period began to be supplemented with various types of auxiliaries. Tangut, Uighur and Khitan mercenaries, both horse and foot, were recruited in increasing numbers. By the time of the Mongol invasions the Chin had also come to rely heavily on native Chinese infantry known as 'chung-hsiao chun' or 'loyal and filial' troops, who presumably fought mainly as swordsmen and crossbowmen like those previously recruited by the Liao.

The Battle of Huan-erh-tsui, 1211

The army which the Chin mustered to oppose the Mongols was variously claimed to be 300,000 or 500,000 strong, although as usual both figures must surely be far too high. It included a high proportion of Chinese infantry and Khitan mercenary cavalry as well as mounted Jurchens. Its commander, Ke-shih-lieh Chih-chung, was advised by two of his staff officers to advance rapidly with the cavalry to attack the invaders as they emerged from the Gobi Desert, when their horses would be exhausted and the army would be forced to disperse to allow them to graze. However he was unwilling to fight without his infantry, and so he marched slowly over the mountain passes north of Chung-tu to enable them to keep up. Another Chin army was also moving to support him, but Ke-shih-lieh refused to wait for it to arrive. This has led to the suggestion that he was overconfident and did not regard the Mongols as a serious threat, but if his army was anywhere near as big as the sources claim, he would not have been able to supply any more reinforcements, nor deploy them effectively if they had arrived. In fact the infantry he did take with him played no significant part in the ensuing engagement.

The Chin army emerged from the Yeh-lu Mountains and drew up in line of battle to meet the Mongols at a place known as Huan-erh-tsui, or 'Young Badger's Mouth'. This place was said to be on the very edge of the land of China, where the cultivated country ended and the northern wastes began. From here open grassland and desert sands stretched all the way to Mongolia, making it ideal country for the Mongol mounted archery tactics. Ke-shih-lieh deployed with his cavalry in a long line in front, with the Chinese footsoldiers crowding uselessly behind where their crossbowmen were unable to see the enemy. He sent an emissary to Chinggis Khan to propose terms, but this man apparently changed sides and provided the Mongols with details of the Chin deployment. To counter it Chinggis seems to have employed a classic Mongol tactic known as the 'chisel attack' (Onon). While the bulk of the army pinned the enemy by skirmishing with their bows from a distance, one unit would charge at a specific point in their line, followed by a second unit, and if necessary a third. As soon as one group broke through, the rest of the army would concentrate on a signal and follow it through the gap. This sounds reminiscent of the echeloned attack by squadrons which was pioneered in Europe in the eighteenth century by Frederick the Great, and although we are not specifically told that the Mongols manoeuvred in this way, with units diagonally behind one another, it seems highly likely that they did. The effect would be to allow the attackers to concentrate several units against a single unit of defenders and wear them down with successive charges. But if the Mongols were forced to retire, their opponents could not exploit their advantage, since another Mongol unit was always in position to attack in support.

Whatever the precise method used, the Mongol left wing charged and managed to drive the opposing Jurchen cavalry back, but far from being able to support them the infantrymen behind were unable to advance through their comrades, and in fact were thrown into disorder in their turn as panic-stricken horses stampeded into their ranks. The situation was reminiscent of the climax of the Battle of Ssu-shui (see Chapter 7), where a similar long, continuous line had been unable to manoeuvre in response to controlled charges by smaller but more flexible groups of cavalry. As the Mongols followed up, with the Khan himself and his general Mukhali at their head, the Chin right flank collapsed in rout, with 'men and horses trampling each other down in the rout and the dead being without number'. On witnessing this the rest of the army fled for the passes leading back to Chung-tu, but the Mongols pursued them mercilessly. The Jurchen rallied briefly at Hui Ho Pao, but fled again when they learned that some of the Khitan units in their army were going over to the enemy. Eventually Ke-shih-lieh Chih-chung cut his way out to safety with 7,000 cavalrymen, but the bodies of most of their comrades were left scattered along thirty miles of mountain roads. Ten years later the sage Ch'ang-ch'un and a party of Taoist monks, travelling north to a meeting with Chinggis in Central Asia, found the bones still lying there and organised a belated prayer service for the dead.

The Defences of Chung-tu

In the aftermath of the defeat at Huan-erh-tsui several of the Chin frontier forts surrendered or were betrayed to the Mongols by their Khitan garrisons, but Chung-tu itself continued to hold out, and it is unlikely that at this stage of the campaign Chinggis seriously considered assaulting it. This was not surprising, because the Mongols were still inexperienced in siegecraft, and the Chin capital incorporated all of the lessons of two millennia of Chinese experience in the art of fortification. The walls of the main city were made of rammed earth faced with stone, ten miles round, forty feet high and forty-five feet thick at the base. Every fifty feet or so was a low tower, with a battlemented parapet running between them, while in front of them were three concentric water-filled moats. Beyond the main defences were four outlying forts, each garrisoned by 4,000 men, with underground tunnels connecting them to the city. In addition to the stone-throwers and heavy crossbows available to earlier dynasties, terrifying new weapons had been added to the Chin arsenal. Some time in the late T'ang period Chinese alchemists, paradoxically in search of the elixir of youth, had discovered the explosive properties of a primitive form of gunpowder. The earliest treatise to mention the substance does so as a warning not to experiment with it, but during the tenth century the formula was gradually refined and applied to military purposes. Among these were incendiary arrows, hand-hurled grenades, and impregnated slow matches for igniting flamethrowers, the latter using naphtha probably imported from the Middle East by Arab traders. A Sung military manual known as the *Wu Ching Tsung Yao*, first published in 1044, describes a brass flamethrower which could be mounted on the ramparts of a city, and employed double-acting bellows to produce a continuous stream of flaming naphtha. This might be used either directly against attackers trying to climb the wall, or to spread burning oil on the surface of a moat. The same Sung source also mentions gunpowder 'bombs' thrown by rope-powered artillery, though these had soft casings made of paper or bamboo and so were incendiaries rather than true high-explosive bombs, intended perhaps to burn siege engines and frighten opponents who were not accustomed to them, rather than to actually kill people. Another gunpowder device which was probably available to the defenders of Chung-tu was the fire-lance or 'huo-ch'iang' which in its simplest form was a personal weapon resembling a roman candle on the end of a stick, with or without a spear point as backup. Once lit, the fire-lance shot smoke and flames to a range of up to ten paces, which must have been sufficient to keep most opponents at a distance until the charge burned out. Fire-lances are not mentioned in the *Wu Ching Tsung Yao* or other Sung manuals, nor in surviving battle descriptions before the siege of K'ai-feng in 1232, but they are illustrated on a painted silk banner from Tun-huang, in Hsi-Hsia territory, which is now in the

Musée Guimet in Paris and is usually dated to the tenth century. Perhaps they were regarded as a 'secret weapon', but it seems unlikely that the Chin, who had been in contact with both Hsi-Hsia and Sung China for a century, would have been unaware of them. Eventually the fire-lance evolved into something like a primitive gun, which expelled solid projectiles to accompany the flames, but the first written account of this development did not appear until 1259. Later in the thirteenth century the effectiveness of these weapons for siege warfare was often increased by mounting them in large numbers on wheeled frames, which could be

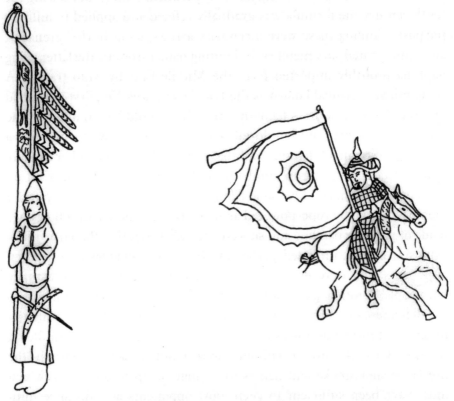

Standard bearers of the T'ang dynasty. At left is an infantry man from a painting in the tomb of Prince Yide, who was buried in AD 706. He appears to carry a sword and a bow in a leopard skin case. At right is a heavy cavalryman taken from a painting from Tun-huang, c. AD 800. Note the lack of horse armour, a concession to mobility which was probably typical of cavalrymen who fought in Central Asia.

quickly pushed into position and ignited simultaneously to stop a rush against a gate or a breach in the walls.

Far more deadly engines of war were certainly under development by the time of the siege of Chung-tu, but unfortunately we cannot be sure that they were used on that occasion. In 1221 the Chin attacked the Sung city of Ch'i-chou, and according to Chao Yu-jung their siege engines shot bottle-shaped bombs with casings made from two-inch thick cast iron, which exploded 'with a noise like thunder' and killed many people (Needham). These appear to have been true fragmentation bombs, using gunpowder with an increased proportion of saltpetre, which was powerful enough to burst the casing and shower the target with jagged pieces of metal like a modern high-explosive shell. The tone of this account suggests that they were a novelty at that time, but whether they had been hastily developed as a response to the failure of the more conventional defences at Chung-tu, or whether they had been in use for some time but the surviving sources fail to mention them, we do not know. In 1231 a Chin fleet used similar missiles against a Mongol army on the Yellow River, and in the following year the Official History of the dynasty describes them in greater detail in its account of the Mongol siege of K'ai-feng. The explosion of one of these 'chien-t'ien-lei' or 'heaven-shaking thunder' bombs could be heard for several miles, and would devastate an area of 'more than half a mou', which corresponds very roughly to a square sixty feet on each side. They were said to be able to penetrate even iron armour, presumably with pieces of the casing acting as shrapnel. The Mongols tried to counter them by advancing under the cover of sheets of ox hide, but the Chin began to let down the bombs on the end of iron chains, so that they would explode under the hides or in the besiegers' trenches. The Mongols, we are told, 'were all blown to bits, not even a trace being left behind'. These bombs, and 'flying-fire spears', were said to be the only weapons that the Mongols were afraid of. The 'flying-fire spears' are usually regarded as a variety of hand-held fire-lance, but the possibility that they were longer-ranged missiles propelled by gunpowder cannot be discounted. Nevertheless the Mongols eventually took K'ai-feng, so these technical advances were obviously no more decisive there than they had been at Chung-tu.

The Barbarians Break Through

Rather surprisingly, in view of their own 'barbarian' origin and tradition of mounted warfare, the Chin had enthusiastically adopted the Chinese practice of building long defensive walls to protect the settled country against invaders from the steppe. Their linear walls, however, were no more effective than those of their predecessors had been, and were built at the usual terrible cost in money and lives. A song of this period laments that if the bones of those who died during the construction of one such barrier had been left in place, they would have formed an obstacle as high as the wall itself. And yet it is clear from the manoeuvres of the Mongol armies that although the strategic passes were commanded by forts, they were not blocked by anything resembling the Great Wall as we know it today.

During the winter of 1211 to 1212 the Mongols streamed through the gaps in the Chin border defences, thrusting deep into north China in several widely separated columns. It is clear that they were not afraid of being defeated in detail by the surviving Chin field armies, but this campaign was more of a massive pillaging expedition than a serious attempt to conquer territory. Chinggis himself rode two hundred miles south to the Yellow River, while another army under Jebei thrust eastwards into the Chin heartland in what is now Manchuria. Here it is said that he captured the capital city at Mukden (modern Shenyang), not by conventional siege operations but by a typical Mongol trick. After a failed probing attack against the walls, his army abandoned most of its baggage and plunder outside the city and retreated in apparent disorder. By the time of the New Year celebrations they were a hundred miles away, and when their patrols reported this, the people of Mukden thought it was safe to open the gates and begin to collect the loot. But this took time, and a Mongol army could ride a hundred miles in the course of a day and a night, making use of relays of spare ponies. Jebei also had scouts out, and when he learned of what was happening he returned unexpectedly to find the gates still open. Following the panic-stricken citizens into the city, he sacked it and rode off again to present its riches to his Khan.

The invaders then withdrew to the steppes, only to return briefly in the autumn, when Chinggis called off the campaign temporarily while he recovered from an arrow wound. But in 1213 they were back, and this time their objective was conquest as well as plunder. The Chin had reoccupied the pass at Huan-erh-tsui, but Jebei managed to take the fort at its northern end. Accounts of how he did this differ: *The Secret History* describes a feigned flight similar to that employed at Mukden, but according to the Official History of the Yuan dynasty the fort was handed over by a treacherous Chin officer. However the Mongols pressed on across the mountains to the fortress at Chu-yung, which was only twenty miles from Chung-tu. Chinggis Khan's generals bypassed the main defences by following a narrow path through the mountains which had been revealed to them by a Muslim merchant named Ja'far. Ja'far's eagerness to help the invaders was apparently due to the fact that he had been wrongly imprisoned by the Chin authorities as a suspected Mongol spy, although it seems equally likely that he had been a spy from the beginning. Chu-yung was captured, as was another fortress at the Chi-ching Pass, which had been held by a garrison under Ke-shih-lieh Chih-chung, the defeated commander at Huan-erh-tsui. What happened here is unclear. Ke-shih-lieh apparently evacuated the position without orders, allowing a Mongol army to advance through the pass and surprise a Chin field army led by a general named Wa-yen Kang. On their return to the capital Kang accused his colleague of treason. Ke-shih-lieh denied the charge, but was afraid that the Emperor Wei-shou would believe his accuser and have him executed. He therefore staged a coup, killed the emperor and five hundred of his bodyguards, and appointed himself regent, ruling Chung-tu on behalf of his own nominee.

Two months later the Mongols appeared outside the walls of Chung-tu, and the city's new ruler despatched an officer named Kao-ch'i with only 6,000 men to fight a delaying action. Kao-ch'i had apparently been a longstanding rival of Ke-shih-lieh, and this suicidal mission may have been deliberately intended to get rid of him. If so it did not work. Kao-ch'i led his men against the regent's palace, beheaded him, and proclaimed himself regent and commander-in-chief in his place. Meanwhile the Mongols again bypassed Chung-tu in three columns and ravaged the rural districts as far as the Yellow River. One column, under Jochi, marched south down the valley of the Fen River and took the cities of Ping-yang, Fen-chou and T'ai-yuan, while another went east down the Yellow River to Teng-chou on the north coast of the Shantung Peninsula – probably the first occasion on which Chinggis Khan's armies saw the sea. Everywhere they went they burned villages, destroyed crops and left behind total devastation. By the beginning of 1214 only seven towns north of the great river still held out for the Chin, and the scorched earth policy was beginning to have its effect on Chung-tu itself, where the extravagant feasts for which Ke-shih-lieh Chih-chung had been notorious, were giving way to famine. But the Mongols were suffering almost as badly. In the aftermath of the successful raids their confidence had soared, and they petitioned Chinggis for permission to storm the city. Reluctantly he allowed the attempt, which was beaten off with heavy losses. Meanwhile the Tanguts of Hsi-Hsia, who had been vassals of the Mongols since 1209, sent an army of 80,000 men against the Chin, only to suffer a crushing defeat at the Battle of Lin-t'ao. It was at this point in the campaign that John de Plano Carpini alleges that Chinggis had to order one man in every ten to be killed so that the rest could eat his flesh. This lurid tale is of course highly unlikely, but it does illustrate the reputation which the Mongols were earning for both ruthlessness and discipline.

In fact, rather than eat his own soldiers, the Khan opened negotiations with the Chin. His messengers informed Kao-ch'i that the Chin were now so weak that the Mongols feared incurring the wrath of Heaven if they took advantage of their distress. Instead Chinggis was prepared to go home and leave them in peace, in exchange for a token tribute to keep his hungry soldiers happy. Terms were agreed, and the Mongols rode off northwards to graze their ponies on the shores of the lake known as Dohon Nor, on the steppes south of the Gobi, taking with them a haul of booty which included 3,000 horses, 10,000 bolts of silk and 500 slaves. Kao-chi, however, did not regard the agreement as more than a temporary respite, and he realised that in the long run Chung-tu could not be held while the Mongols were able to ravage its hinterland with such impunity. He therefore decided to move the court to a place of safety in the south, and in the summer of 1214 he and his puppet emperor set out at the head of an immense train of 30,000 wagons for K'ai-feng, the former capital of the Northern Sung, on the southern shore of the Yellow River. However 2,000 Khitan cavalrymen who were ordered to accompany them refused to abandon their own homeland, and instead defected to the Mongols. When they informed Chinggis Khan of the move he was – or pretended to be – shocked at the implication that the Chin did not trust him. Declaring that he had been tricked, he ordered an immediate resumption of the siege of Chung-tu.

The Fall of Chung-tu

At the same time Mukhali was sent east to complete the conquest of Manchuria. Here the remaining Chin garrisons were isolated and increasingly demoralised, while the Khitan inhabitants of much of the country were openly pro-Mongol. In the spring of 1215 the city of Liao-yang was captured with the aid of a Khitan officer named Shi-mo Yesen, who informed Mukhali that a new commander was on his way from K'ai-feng to take over the garrison. So an ambush was laid, and the Chin officer was intercepted and killed. Shi-mo then took his written authority and, using his knowledge of Jurchen military procedures, managed to get into Liao-yang and pass himself off as the new commander. He ordered all the sentries on the walls to stand down and then opened the gates, so that the Mongols entered the city without a fight.

Meanwhile the garrison of Chung-tu had been left under the command of an officer named Wan-yen Fu-hing, who appears to have waited passively while the enemy surrounded the walls and intercepted two uncoordinated relief expeditions sent from K'ai-feng. They were both defeated north of Ho-ch'ien, and the desperately needed supplies of food which they brought with them were commandeered by the Mongols. By this time a Khitan contingent under Ming-Ngan had arrived to reinforce the besiegers with infantry and siege engines, but in the event an assault was not necessary. The Mongol operations in the surrounding countryside had left the city isolated and without hope of resupply, and as the citizens starved their leaders turned on each other in violent recriminations. The civilian governor killed himself, and Wan-yen Fu-hing abandoned his men and escaped to K'ai-feng, where he was accused of treason and beheaded. One day in May 1215 – apparently at the instigation of a Chin defector – the inhabitants opened the gates and allowed the Mongols into the city without a fight.

Chinggis was not present at the time; he had handed over command of the Chinese front to Mukhali and was actually on his way back to

Mongolia when the city fell. However it is hard to believe that the outcome would have been very different if he had been personally in charge. The Mongols had fought a hard campaign, and both they and their Khitan allies had bitter memories of what they saw as Jurchen treachery and oppression. In any case their main motive for being in China at all was plunder, and Chung-tu was rich beyond their wildest dreams. They systematically looted the city, then set fire to it. The loss of life must have been considerable, even though, as happened countless times during the Mongol conquests, rumour and deliberate propaganda soon inflated the figure to unbelievable proportions. In 1216 a mission arrived from Khwarizmia, allegedly to confirm whether a city as strong as Chung-tu could really have been captured by a horde of barbarians, as had been reported. The ambassador saw for himself the piles of skeletons still lying unburied, and witnessed a typhus epidemic said to have been caused by the decomposing corpses of the citizens, but the account he received of 60,000 young women throwing themselves from the walls to avoid capture must have been wildly exaggerated. Certainly the city cannot have been totally destroyed or depopulated, since Li Chin-ch'ang, one of the followers of the Taoist sage Ch'ang-ch'un, recorded that the holy man was delayed by the welcome staged by crowds of priests and devotees when he passed through in 1221.

Mongol China and its Aftermath

The capture of Chung-tu established the young Mongol Empire as a power to be reckoned with, but it took another twenty years to finally destroy the Chin. In 1216 an army crossed the Yellow River and threatened K'ai-feng, but was forced to withdraw. Then three years later Chinggis led his armies west for an extended campaign against the Khwarizmian Empire, leaving Mukhali to finish the conquest of northern China. Short-sightedly, the Sung in the south then stabbed the hated Jurchens in the back instead of supporting them as a buffer against the Mongols; in 1217 they had ceased paying the tribute that was due under the terms of the peace of 1141, and two years later they attacked and overran most of Shantung Province. In 1222 a Sung army under P'eng I-pin even marched into Mongol-held territory, only to be defeated and captured at the Battle of Tsan-huang in 1225. Chinggis died in 1227 while fighting the Tanguts, who had defied him by refusing to supply troops for the war in Khwarizmia, but his successor Ogotai continued to pursue the feud with the Chin. By now the Mongols were able to call on large numbers of Chinese infantry recruited from the conquered provinces in the north, as well as siege engines and skilled technicians to operate them. By contrast the Chin, fighting on two fronts, were never able to recover from the loss of Chung-tu. In 1232 K'ai-feng finally fell to a two-pronged attack from the north and west, and three years after that the last Chin emperor hanged himself.

The Sung were now left without allies against the vengeful Mongols. It is unlikely that Chinggis had ever contemplated such an ambitious project as the conquest of the whole of China, but by this time the long campaign had developed a momentum of its own. Nevertheless the Southern Sung Empire was still the richest and most populous state in the world, and it was another forty years before its capital, Hang-chou, finally fell to Chinggis' grandson Kubilai Khan. In less than eighty years the Mongols had established the largest land empire in history, and come closer than anyone before or since to realising the age-old dream of ruling the entire globe. They had conquered all but the remotest outer reaches of the Eurasian continent, overthrown almost everyone who dared to oppose them, and set world history on a course which it still follows today. At one point they had planned and executed the simultaneous invasions of Poland and Korea – something which even Stalin never attempted. But after Kubilai's death their impetus was spent. The Yuan dynasty which he founded in China undertook no new conquests. Chinggis' descendants in Western Asia settled down and adopted the religion of their Muslim subjects, while those remaining in their old heartland dissipated their energies in an endless series of civil wars. Opposition to the Mongols had crystallised around two remarkable military states founded by Turkish slave-soldiers – the Sultanate of Delhi and the Mamluks of Egypt. The year 1299 saw a Mongol victory over each of these enemies, but these victories were almost the very last. Gradually their victims began to organise themselves and fight back. In 1351 an army of forced labourers collected by the Yuan regime for flood control projects on the Yellow River took up arms and sparked off a rebel movement known as the Red

Turbans, who quickly drove the Mongols out of south China. By 1368 a talented war leader named Chu Yuan-chang had reunified most of the country, and in September of that year Ta-tu, the capital which Kubilai had built on the site of Jurchen Chung-tu, was finally back in Chinese hands.

Chapter Eleven

Conclusion: The Chinese and Western Military Traditions – Contrast or Convergence?

The native dynasty which Chu Yuan-chang founded became known as the Ming, or 'Brilliant', but it remained inward-looking, perhaps in reaction against the traumas of the Mongol invasions, and it never equalled the conquests of the Han or the T'ang. It was the Ming who built the Great Wall as we know it today, in an attempt to protect the empire against further incursions from the steppe. Nevertheless, in 1644 the dynasty was overthrown by a new wave of invaders from the north, the Manchus, who had been allowed through the Wall to help one of the factions in a civil war. Drawing on their own tradition of cavalry warfare, the Manchus took the offensive against the nomads of Central Asia, and during the eighteenth century they expanded the empire to its widest ever extent. But by this time they were falling behind in the technological race with the newly industrialising powers of Europe. The nineteenth century saw the humiliation of the Manchu armed forces in the Opium Wars, and China entered a long period of relative decline, from which it is only now emerging.

It can be argued that even after they had been thrown out of China and reduced to their former status as wandering 'barbarian' tribes, the Mongols had continued to influence the course of Chinese history. The campaigns of Pan Chao and Kao Hsien-chih had seen faltering first attempts at establishing links with the rest of the Eurasian continent, but it was the Mongol Empire that finally brought about regular contacts between what until then had been two separate worlds. The Chinese and European military traditions now began to converge. It was thanks to the Mongols that Chinese gunpowder reached Europe, eventually to revolutionise warfare there, and when the short-lived *pax Mongolica* collapsed, it was gun-armed ships from Europe that sought out other routes to the riches of the Far East, giving rise to the global civilisation that we see today.

Ultimately the Chinese were neither more nor less successful than contemporary Europeans: they were neither the unwarlike victims of a succession of conquerors, nor the possessors of secret knowledge which made them unbeatable. In the contemporary west the 'Oriental art of war' exemplified by Sun Tzu and other writers is often regarded as holding the key to success in every sphere from present day military strategy to business negotiations. However its emphasis on 'knowing yourself and knowing your enemy', and using that knowledge to manipulate events, does not represent an entirely separate tradition, but had its equivalent in the work of Greek, Roman and other western strategists. Both were trying to codify an approach to warfare which relies heavily on a commander's flexibility in responding to particular situations, rather than following a rigid set of procedures, and it is this approach that has brought success to the most intelligent commanders from all cultures and in all ages.

When military developments in east and west are compared, there were few if any time periods in which either would have had a decisive technological advantage. The first great Chinese invention in the field of weapons technology was the crossbow, introduced in the fifth or fourth century BC, but the Greeks were using a similar device at about the same time, and though it never became a mainstay of their field armies as it did in Warring States and Han China, the heavier versions designed for siege warfare developed more or less in parallel in east and west. As we have seen, the characteristic offensive weapon of most of the great imperial dynasties was a foreign invention – the Central Asian composite bow. China's best known indigenous contribution to warfare, gunpowder, was used for limited military applications from the tenth century AD, but it took many years to discover the formula for a truly explosive mixture, and until the thirteenth century it was basically an incendiary rather than a high explosive weapon – a slightly improved version of Greek Fire and the naphtha bombs already in use in the Middle East. True guns did not appear until the end of the thirteenth century, only a few years before their arrival in Europe, although the fact that the formula for explosive gunpowder appears ready made in the west, without repeating the long experimental process seen earlier in China, suggests that the European developments were not indigenous but were inspired by, if not directly copied from, Chinese prototypes. The spectacular rocket batteries which are so often associated with Chinese armies were an even later invention, not appearing in battle accounts until the late fourteenth century, by which time European gun-founding technology was already forging ahead. Despite the undoubted inventiveness of Chinese civilisation, its ancient and medieval fighting men essentially won their battles in the same way as the rest of the world, by the strength of human and animal muscle, allied to ingenuity and courage. It is for this that they deserve to be remembered.

Sources and Further Reading

Primary Sources in Translation:

Boyle, J. *Ata Malik Juvaini: The History of the World Conqueror*, Harvard University Press, 1958.

Crump, J. *Chan-kuo Ts'e*, Clarendon Press, 1970.

Dawson, R. *Sima Qian: The First Emperor – Selections from the Historical Records*, Oxford University Press, 2007.

Dubs, H. *The History of the Former Han Dynasty*, Kegan Paul, Trench, Trubner & Co, 1944.

Griffith, S. *Sun Tzu – The Art of War*, Oxford University Press, 1963.

Legge, J. *The Chinese Classics Vol 5: Tso Chuan*, Oxford University Press, 1872.

Loewe, M. *Records of Han Administration* (2 vols), Cambridge University Press, 1967.

Onon, U. *The Secret History of the Mongols: The Life and Times of Chinggis Khan*, Curzon Press, 2001.

des Rotours, R. *Traite des Fonctionnaires et Traite de l'Armee, Traduit de la Nouvelle Histoire des T'ang*, Leiden 1948.

Sawyer, R. *The Seven Military Classics of Ancient China*, Westview Press, Boulder, Colorado, 1993.

Sawyer, R. *Sun Tzu – Art of War*, Westview Press, Boulder, Colorado, 1994.

Sawyer, R. *Sun Pin – Military Methods*, Westview Press, Boulder, Colorado, 1995.

Waley, A (trans) & Allen, J (ed) *The Book of Songs*, New York, 1996.

Wang, Y. *A Record of Buddhist Monasteries in Lo-yang*, Princeton University Press, 1984.

Watson, B. *Records of the Grand Historian of China*, Columbia University Press, 1969.

Secondary Sources:

Ancient Chinese Armour, Shanghai Classics Publishing House, 1996 (Chinese text).

Anthony, D.W. *The Horse, The Wheel and Language*, Princeton University Press, 2007.

Beckwith, C. *The Tibetan Empire in Central Asia*, Princeton University Press, 1987.

Blunden, C. & Elvin, M. *Cultural Atlas of China*, Phaidon, 1983.

The Cambridge History of China, Vol. 1: The Ch'in and Han Empires, Cambridge University Press, 1986.

The Cambridge History of China, Vol. 3: Sui and T'ang China, 589 – 906, Cambridge University Press, 1979.

The Cambridge History of China, Vol. 6: Alien Regimes and Border States, 907 – 1368, Cambridge University Press, 1994.

Chang, K. *Shang Civilisation*, Yale University Press, 1980.

Cottrell, A. *The First Emperor of China*, Macmillan, 1981.

Desmond Martin, H. *The Rise of Chingis Khan and his Conquest of North China*, Johns Hopkins Press, Baltimore, 1950.

Diamond, J. *Guns, Germs and Steel: The Fates of Human Societies*, London, 1997.

Dien, A. *A Study of Early Chinese Armour, Artibus Asiae XLIII 1/2*, 1981-82.

Dien, A. *The Stirrup and its Effect on Chinese Military History*, Ars Orientalis XVI, University of Michigan, 1987.

Fitzgerald, C. *Son of Heaven: A Biography of Li Shih-min, Founder of the T'ang Dynasty*, Cambridge University Press, 1933.

Franck, I. & Brownstone. D. *The Silk Road, A History, Facts on File Publications*, New York, 1986.

Gernet, J. *Ancient China from the Beginnings to the Empire*, Faber & Faber, 1968.

de Hartog, L. *Genghis Khan, Conqueror of the World*, London, 1989.

Hsiao, C. *The Military Establishment of the Yuan Dynasty*, Harvard University Press, 1978.

Hulsewe, A. *China in Central Asia, The Early Stage, 125 BC–AD 23*, E.J. Brill, 1979.

Jenner, W. *Memories of Lo-yang: Yang Hsuan-chih and the Lost Capital,* Oxford University Press, 1981.

Karasulas, A. *Mounted Archers of the Steppe, 600 BC–AD 1300,* Osprey Elite Series Vol. 120, Oxford, 2004.

Kierman, F. & Fairbank, J. *Chinese Ways in Warfare,* Harvard University Press, 1974.

Lau, D. & Ames, R. *Sun Pin: The Art of Warfare,* Ballantine Books, New York, 1993.

Loewe, M. *Military Operations in the Han Period,* China Society Occasional Papers No. 12, The China Society, 1961.

Lovell, J. *The Great Wall: China Against the World, 1000 BC–AD 2000,* Atlantic Books, London, 2006.

Mackerras, C. *The Uighur Empire,* Canberra, 1972.

Man, J. *Genghis Khan, Life, Death and Resurrection,* Transworld Publishers, London, 2011.

Morgan, D. *The Mongols,* Oxford, 1986.

Needham, J. *Science and Civilisation in China Vol. 5, Part 7: The Gunpowder Epic,* Cambridge University Press, 1989.

Nicolle, D. *The Mongol Warlords,* Firebird Books, Poole, Dorset, 1990.

Payne-Gallwey, Sir R. *The Crossbow,* London, 1903.

Peers, C. *Warlords of China, 700 BC–AD 1662,* Arms & Armour Press, 1998.

Peers, C. *Soldiers of the Dragon: Chinese Armies 1500 BC–AD 1840,* Osprey Publishing, 2006.

Piggott, S. *Wagon, Chariot and Carriage: Symbolism and Status in the History of Transport,* London, 1992

Pope, S. *Bows and Arrows,* University of California, 1962.

Pulleyblank, E. *The Background of the Rebellion of An Lu-shan,* Oxford University Press, 1955.

Ranitsch, K-H. *The Army of Tang China,* Montvert Publications, Stockport, 1995.

Ratchnevsky, P. *Genghis Khan, His Life and Legacy,* London, 1991.

Rawson, J. *Ancient China, Art and Archaeology,* British Museum Publications, 1980.

Rudolph, R. *The Minatory Crossbowman in Early Chinese Tombs,* Archives of the Chinese Art Society of America, Vol. XIX, 1965.

Russell Robinson, H. *Oriental Armour,* Herbert Jenkins, 1967.

Schafer, E. *The Vermilion Bird*, University of California Press, 1967.

Skoljar, S. *L'Artillerie de Jet a l'Epoque Sung*, Etudes Song series 1. Vol. 2, Sorbonne, 1971.

Tao, J. *The Jurchen in Twelfth-Century China: A Study of Sinicization*, University of Washington, 1976.

Turnbull, S. *Siege Weapons of the Far East 1*, Osprey Vanguard Series Vol. 43, Oxford, 2001.

Turnbull, S. *Siege Weapons of the Far East 2*, Osprey Vanguard Series Vol. 44, Oxford, 2002.

Turnbull, S. *The Great Wall of China*, Osprey Fortress Series Vol. 57, Oxford, 2007.

Turnbull, S. *Chinese Walled Cities, 221 BC to AD 1644*, Osprey Fortress Series Vol. 84, Oxford, 2012.

Waldron, A. *The Great Wall of China*, Cambridge University Press, 1990.

Walker, R. L. *The Multi-State System of Ancient China*, Shoestring Press, Connecticut, 1953.

Yang Hong, *Weapons in Ancient China*, Science Press, Beijing & New York, 1992.

Index